Beyond Disaster

Critical Insurgencies

This series interrogates what it means to do critical ethnic studies work within, outside, and across a variety of locations, from within the academy and community organizing spaces, to the arts and media, mass movements, intimate spaces, and beyond. Since theory and practice reside in multiple geographies and through multiple genres of work, Critical Insurgencies engages diverse readerships and generates conversations that resist the ways that ethnic studies work can be limited by the historical separation between academic writing and public-facing texts.

Critical Insurgencies publishes interdisciplinary scholarship that acknowledges and articulates the undeniable connections between race, gender, sexuality, class, religion, and indigeneity as they are deployed to distort, erase, oppress, and exploit vulnerable populations. Books in the series forge new theoretical and political practices for academics and independent scholars in a range of disciplines, activist spaces, and research-based methodologies. We seek manuscripts that work to trouble the nation-state, neoliberalism, carcerality, settler colonialism, and Western hegemony, as well as heteropatriarchal racial formations, sexual and gender binaries, and ableism: books that challenge all forms of oppression and state violence to imagine more generative futures.

Series Editors: Jodi A. Byrd and Michelle M. Wright

Beyond Disaster

Building Collective Futures in Puerto Rico

Melissa L. Rosario

Northwestern University Press
Evanston, Illinois

Northwestern University Press
www.nupress.northwestern.edu

Printed in the United States of America

10   9   8   7   6   5   4   3   2   1

Library of Congress Cataloging-in-Publication Data

Names: Rosario, Melissa L., author.
Title: Beyond disaster : building collective futures in Puerto Rico / Melissa L
    Rosario.
Other titles: Critical insurgencies.
Description: Evanston : Northwestern University Press, 2025. | Series:
    Critical insurgencies | Includes bibliographical references and index.
Identifiers: LCCN 2024039849 | ISBN 9780810146730 (paperback) | ISBN
    9780810146747 (cloth) | ISBN 9780810146754 (ebook)
Subjects: LCSH: Ethnology—Puerto Rico. | Puerto Rico—Social
    conditions—21st century. | Puerto Rico—Colonial influence.
Classification: LCC HN233.5 .R68 2025 | DDC 306.097295—dc23/
    eng/20240828

LC record available at https://lccn.loc.gov/2024039849

 Knowledge Unlatched

An electronic version of this book is freely available, thanks to the support of
libraries working with Knowledge Unlatched. KU is a collaborative initiative
designed to make high-quality books open access for the public good. More
information about the initiative and links to the open-access version can be
found at www.knowledgeunlatched.org.

CONTENTS

ACKNOWLEDGMENTS

This work would never have been possible without the support of community, and my loving ancestors and guides who help me enter the flow of divine intelligence again and again. I offer a big bow of gratitude to my partner Lau Pat R.A., who has always been my biggest supporter and knows the struggles I faced to complete this creative work. Lau, thank you for affirming me in moments when I felt unsure. I hope this work is infused with your gift for capturing the complexity and beauty of life. Thank you, Kehaulani, for helping me to write a book proposal at the very end of my time at Wesleyan. Without this initial plan, I may never have found the motivation to finish this book. Thank you, Candida Gonzalez, for paying for a newspaper subscription so I could access articles hidden beyond a paywall. Thank you, Charis Boke, for sending copies of new research articles, for facilitating and recording a healing justice conversation with *el equipo estelar* and generally being a great friend over the years. Thank you, David and Margie Rosario, for always believing in me even when you did not fully understand me. Thank you, Sandra and Israel of Sandra Farms, for sharing the cloud haven with me and for the delicious homegrown coffee and chocolate. Thank you, Yasmin Hernandez, for asynchronous conversations over voice notes about the rematriation journey. Thank you, Gina Ulysse, for your mentorship and friendship over the last twenty years. You have always inspired me to be bold and live with integrity. Thank you, Giovanni, Paola, Marisel, mulowayi, mapenzi, Ana Elisa, Jorge, Xiomara, Jessica, and Lau, for offering me your time and energy to create the microhistories in part 2. Each of you motivate me to walk this path toward collective liberation. Thank you, Abuela Kukuya, for blessing this work and for sharing your wisdom in ceremony and life. Thank you, the good people at Northwestern University Press, for seeing this to completion. When Gianna Francesca Mosser sent me an email after Hurricane Maria to offer me an indefinite extension, I felt supported in a way I didn't think possible from a publisher. I am equally grateful to her successor Faith Wilson Stein for the guidance and unwavering encouragement she offered once I picked up the manuscript again. I also thank Michelle Wright and Jodi Byrd, the series editors, for their insightful comments on a later version of the manuscript that helped me take on the hard questions and be upfront about my commitments. Finalmente, doy mi más profundo agradecimiento a Atabey por haberme llamado de vuelta a la tierra Boriké. Y doy mi gratitud por ti Guabancex, quien me inició en el camino rojo. A todes les guardianes de esta tierra, las fuerzas de los elementos; gracias. Hahõbaná Guatauba—gracias por llenar mis palabras de sabiduría y honra—Hahõbaná Maquetaurie Guayaba—gracias por permitirme renacer dia tras dia—Hahõbaná Yocahú Bagua Maórocoti por alimentar la vida en todo momento.

The Heart Space

To get beyond disaster go to the center. At times this is a literal place: the eye of a storm or the core of the body. At others it is a mystical place—the calm clarity of an open heart or the spiritual center of peace and groundedness. Once at the center, it is possible to approach endings with grace and ease. Worries decrease and pain subsides in the wonderful respite of this space. From the center point change is possible.

Finding the refuge of the center can be difficult, let alone the energy necessary to build collective futures. I am intimately aware of this struggle even as I am convinced that is the only struggle worth undertaking. The center place of my beloved Boriké has continually offered me the medicine to keep going. The land here is as red as I have ever seen it and its vibrancy energizes my body. The vast majority of Puerto Rico's 224 rivers emerge from the heart of Boriké, *la cordillera central* (the central mountain range). The cold and pure waters feed the earth and my spirit.

Yet I've been told that the waters are already beginning to dry. The reserves are full of sediments. The government (insular and federal) and private entities take and take. Even in these magical oases scattered across the archipelago where folks are actively building ecological lives and systems, the water does not easily flow. The time for life as we know it is running out. The elders suggest we spend as much time in the woods as possible to sharpen our understanding of the medicine, a practice that is even more urgent in these times of extinction.

In Jayuya I am gifted a respite at Camp Tabonuco in a small solar-powered cabin made of reclaimed wood. Here I easily fall into the rhythm of the earth and wake before dawn and to bed after sunset. I sleep with the window open, and the moon wakes me. I climb down the ladder and find the door blown open by a sudden gust of wind. I spend part of the night outside with the lights off listening to the star beings, owls, and coquis. I wonder how I could return to the simplicity of the night sky and the morning dew in the busy city of San Juan. What would it take to give up a little bit of our comfort to really be present?

Until I die I pray to increase my capacity for presence, gratitude, and honesty. I will strive to honor what is here in all its beauty and mystery and in all the difficulty. May it remind me to be responsible for what is mine and let the rest dissolve into the wisdom of spirit. I offer this book to these things.

With love, Meli

Beyond Disaster

Another Country

The right of return is a given for Puerto Ricans living in the diaspora. We are not considered refugees or immigrants—a distinctive and ironic privilege conferred on a people whose lands are a possession of, but are not a part of, the empire who claimed them. After two generations and thirty-plus years of my own life, I claimed that right. I was motivated by a personal longing to craft an alternative space of knowledge exchange and practice outside the bounds of academia and a desire to contribute to building collective futures alongside others who were willing to give up the many privileges we could find living elsewhere to fight for this archipelago. This book is the product of the first seven years of my journey.

Shaped from within the crucible of debt restructuring and false promises, in this text I investigate our responsibility to collective liberation. I know that responsibility is a loaded term, given its appropriation by neoliberal governance structures who use it to transfer the failings of the state to individuals. Against this logic, I define responsibility as the ability to respond to and alchemize the conditions, structures, and practices that maintain the order of the world. These responses will always emerge from each person's unique and individual context, but they will not bring about transformation unless they are also crafted in relationship to the collective.

Given my primary interest in tracing shared pathways to action and freedom, I will repeatedly invoke "we" in this text. I am referring principally to anyone who sees their own future bound up with the liberation of Boriké and to those who are willing to be coconspirators in this struggle.[1] I am increasingly aware that the work I hope to do is impossible alone, so in using we, I am inviting you, dear reader, into this dilemma. This "we" may resonate most with other Puerto Ricans, especially fellow rematriators, but I hope that it speaks more widely to activists, artists, and healers, who are invested in solidarity and organizing grounded in ethics and personal responsibility regardless of their background.

As a queer mixed-race person of Puerto Rico's diaspora who rematriated to their ancestral lands, my perspective is at the margins of multiple intersections.[2] As a cultural worker committed to liberation, my work is grounded in the practice of embodiment.[3] My journey of return is a living commitment to transforming this archipelago and is inseparable from the story contained within these pages. I hope that by examining my experience as a rematriator alongside activist worldbuilding efforts to foster collective futures offers a new story of Puerto Rico, a story beyond the framework of debt, disaster, and colonization.[4] In this way I am joining the call made by Haitian American scholar and artist Gina Ulysse whose work offers a more complex vision of her homeland than popular representations of Haiti, which routinely dehumanizes and simplifies the political context. Through short op-ed style pieces, published in English, Kreyòl, and French, Ulysse presents us with multiple and sharp explorations of the Haitian reality after the 2010 earthquake. Similarly, in *Beyond Disaster* I am after a heartfelt and emotive narrative that could shift how we tell the story of our homeland in a way that affirms its complexity and its agency. While Ulysse's work came out rather quickly—all pieces written in a two-year span, this book was slow to materialize.

In fact, this book has been a tremendously long process in the making for a few reasons worth naming here. First, and perhaps most obviously, in leaving academia, I fell out of rhythm with the practice of attending conferences, publishing, and the like. I wrote this work without the benefit of writing workshops or the circles of scholars, friends, or other researchers reading what I wrote.

I also lost access to research being published after leaving a formal academic position. Since no system of public libraries exists in Puerto Rico, it was challenging to keep up-to-date with ongoing debates. Even though I maintain relationships with people who hold academic positions willing to share their login information with me so I might access digital PDFs of new work, universities' increasingly strict verification processes made it very difficult for others to do so. The lack of public access to academic research continues to astound me and to affirm its insularity. Rather than serve a larger public, the practice of gatekeeping in the name of protecting intellectual labor, by and large, only serves a very privileged demographic. Even the University of Puerto Rico, a public institution, offers very little access to materials for those who are not affiliated with an institution or are themselves members of the institution. Consequently, this work is not as densely populated with new research as it would have been if I had not left academia.

What's more, after moving to the archipelago, I began to shape a new organization, the Center for Embodied Pedagogy and Action (CEPA). CEPA represented my effort to take the theories I studied into a practice-based container that could create a new reality for myself and my community on the ground. While I consciously chose to rematriate, I was in no way prepared for the work of building a new institution. I had little understanding of the implications this move would have on my life. I spent lots of time and energy trying to figure out how to grow a life within the context of widespread abandonment. I was uninsured, with little savings, no salary, and chronic pain. It was a struggle to find reasonable rents, and since all my family left Boriké generations ago, I relied on the support of friends and allies who offered me rooms to stay for low cost or trade. I do not exaggerate when I say that I was quite literally struggling to survive.

To complicate matters, just a few days after my first anniversary of living in Puerto Rico, Hurricane Maria hit the island. I set the manuscript down and focused most of my energy on what was right in front of me. I participated in brigades to repair and rebuild. There was great clarity at this time as the myth that US intervention had improved things for Puerto Ricans unraveled. The urgency of healing from trauma and finding the tools to embrace the times we were living in was palpable. The contrast between the deep and miraculous forms of solidarity that emerged locally and in the diaspora alongside the horrific conditions of abandonment and betrayal that left many for dead was shocking. I began hosting spaces to support others to move through the trauma of the moment, resist misery, and heal. CEPA began here: sharing basic techniques to move emotions, return to the body, rest, and imagine while sitting in circle and witnessing each other. As I developed collective models of care and safety in collaboration with so many others, we were shifting the culture of resistance. We were moving beyond disaster in the midst of it.

I continued to return to this manuscript in fits and starts over the course of five years.[5] These compositional challenges shifted my understanding of what I could offer the world through this text. I have done my best to surrender to form, crafting a multigenre text that responds to the different roles I occupy in society: visionary, healing justice practitioner, and cultural worker. Rather than only understanding cultural traditions and patterns—arguably my role as a person trained in anthropology—I consider myself to be part of an ongoing effort to build collective futures and therefore anchor new practices and patterns into being. As a result, it is impossible to fit this work into a single lineage, let alone discipline or area of study. It has been shaped by distinct conversations, within both scholarly and activist communities. Each contains a stream of wisdom that has fed my understanding of the work of collective liberation.

Emergence was key for me as a scholar of social movements, and later, as a practitioner of healing justice. Emergence was a key theoretical ground for understanding the forms of social unrest provoked by the 2008 US financial crisis, bankruptcy, and debt more broadly alongside the spreading of austerity policies worldwide. In the face of ever deepening forms of suffering, a diverse array of resistances emerged globally: the Arab Spring; 15M, also known as the *indignados* movement in Spain; global student strikes (of which Puerto Rico's system-wide strike in 2010 was one); and the rise of the Occupy movement in the United States.[6] Across the world, people were clearly revolting against ever-expanding forms of inequality. Life was too expensive. We were too expendable. It had to end.

Amid a rising sense of uncertainty, organizers began to advocate for making the future we dreamed of in the present moment. Researchers followed suit and used the language of prefiguration to explore the shifting meaning of resistance in the wake of capitalism's failure.[7] My work has been deeply influenced by this shift and explores how practicing new ways of being together offers a pathway toward freedom, even when the alternative is not clear. In the context of Puerto Rico, the debt crisis, and ongoing colonialism, turning toward a smaller scale was freeing. When we turn away from the systems and toward what we are creating at every moment, a bit of our innate power is returned to us.

On a deeper level, emergence has shaped my understanding of the tools and practices that we need to transform oppressive conditions and systems. Fred Moten's work on improvisation within the black tradition suggests that there is a "freedom drive" ever present in the production of cultural works like art and music made by black folx.[8] The technology of improvisation acts as a formal resistance to objectification and helps us to connect to the essence of blackness itself. Although Moten is speaking directly about the context of black music as inextricably linked to the Black radical tradition, there are important parallels to my own. Anyone who has survived a system that disavows their existence knows it requires constant adaptation and creativity.

Improvisation may not be freedom in and of itself, but it represents an important skill we must practice to get free. When in the process of transformation, we inevitably come up against "tight spaces" that require us to quickly adapt.[9] They may be literal spaces like the smallness of a physical space that someone inhabits to escape slavery or war. Or they may be metaphorical spaces like the edge of our comfort zone. In the words of dance scholar Danielle Goldman, improvisation is "a vital technology of the self—an ongoing, critical, physical and anticipatory readiness."[10] Goldman writes at length about the civil rights movement and nonviolent encounters as a kind of improvisation. In this context, improvisation is a product of intense training that allows one to embody a challenge to systems of power through refusal. In my experience living and working in Puerto Rico, so much grace can emerge from how we respond to constriction. Gripping is an embodied response to trauma that traps us in that limitation forced upon us. Slowly working to loosen our grip inside our bodies can open a door to liberation.

Contemporary author adrienne maree brown also worked with emergence to create her now well-known work *Emergent Strategy*. Building on the work of sci-fi black feminist author Octavia Butler and her time working in movement spaces in Detroit, brown articulates the importance of adaptation to the work of social transformation.[11] Drawing from scientific examples, she tracks how relatively simple and small-scale actions lead to complex forms of coordinated action that help species to survive. These emergent behaviors exist only in relation to the group and not individuals alone, as in birds flocking together or bees swarming.[12] Emergence asks us to contemplate the idea that the smallest acts are inseparable from the largest ones and focus our attention there.

Through small gestures of care throughout this text, I attempt a discursive repair from a way of writing and thinking about Puerto Rico that continues to describe the people as victims. I am interested in what is lost when we collapse the complexity of daily life to make a claim about the "disaster" of the colony. While I do agree that Puerto Ricans experience epistemic violence so profoundly it makes living a dignified life extremely challenging on this archipelago, I want to consider the excesses that affirm our persistence and our existence. Kevin Quashie's work on black aliveness is instructive for me.[13] By focusing on the worlds that are created by black authors and poets, Quashie affirms the totality of their aliveness cannot be limited by the historical and present-day violence so often directed at the black body. In other words, Quashie is decentering the conditions of death that are commonplace in the black experience and emphasizing life that escapes all attempts by a white supremacist society to eliminate it. In a similar vein, I am asking, what happens to our understanding of the Puerto Rican condition if we begin by affirming its persistence against over five hundred years of colonization? What parts of us can never been colonized? I think by understanding this aliveness that exceeds all attempts to capture can reinvigorate us in the struggle for collective liberation. This approach is especially vital for those of us choosing to live in Boriké. We need this clarity and cosmic truth to endure and continue to imagine a world beyond the colony.

As a result, I am committed to unpacking the affective dimensions of resistance—how can we feel different—especially when the conditions of life are stifling. Anthropologist Deborah Gould's work on ACT UP also speaks to the role of emotions in social movements. Although her attention is on what could not be felt during direct organizing against the AIDS epidemic, she makes an important intervention in showing how what we feel *moves us,* much more than anything we may logically think or plan.[14] I want to explore here what can't be explained or even seen through debt frameworks. What *does* move us toward collective liberation?

Indeed, although this book began as a counterhistory to debt, I am not particularly interested in the specifics of the debt crisis. Instead, I engage the metaphysics of colonialism to make explicit the ways that everyday Puerto Ricans are forced to pay for a "debt" they did not create, solely by virtue of living in the archipelago itself. As such, this work is existential, embodied, and emotive rather than explanatory.

In the years since completing this work, a plethora of texts have emerged to provide an analysis of how Puerto Rico's $73 billion public debt came to be once it was declared unpayable in 2015 by Governor Alejandro García Padilla in a televised address. I owe a great deal of my understanding of the debt to the deeply politicized work of activist-organizer-researchers like those at LittleSis, Hedge Clippers, and the Committee for Better Banks.[15] Each of these groups helped me to understand who were the key players and what were the loopholes and revolving doors between private and public capital that caused the debt to explode. Rather than understand the moment as a rupture, all research showed that the current crisis was part of a long and ongoing colonial history.[16]

Although the 2006 moment was crucial for understanding the debt's rapid growth, the different mechanisms by which Puerto Rico's economic market is controlled and limited to US markets is far more insidious and long-term. Many can be traced back to the early 1900s. A host of tax havens and exceptions that benefited US corporations have had dire effects on the land and people over time.[17] Of course, Spain and other European powers arrived about four hundred years earlier to the region. They used the people and places they found to expand their empires by mobilizing the strategies of genocide, extraction, pollution, destruction, and enslavement. I suspect that the 1898 moment tends to be emphasized because it is "easier" to trace the origins of Puerto Rico's ongoing "crisis" to US early occupation, and its subsequent legal, political, and economic domination of Puerto Rico.

For those wanting to delve deeper into the origins of the debt crisis, I recommend Rocio Zambrana's *Colonial Debts: The Case of Puerto Rico* as the definitive text. *Colonial Debts* is a highly theoretical treatise engaging with both philosophers writ large and local Puerto Rican scholars, activists, and artists, especially Ariadna Godreau-Aubert, author of *Las propias: Apuntes para una pedagogía de las endeudadas* (Ourselves: Notes for a pedagogy of the indebted woman), founder and executive director of Ayuda Legal.[18] Her focus on *las endeudadas* (the indebted feminine) centers the black, poor, single women who are heads of households and offers a deeply contextual analysis of the way debt is encoded on their bodies. Feminized, racialized, and classed, *las endeudadas* are forced into a kind of no place through the debt. This debt is a trap that places them in a perpetual state of precarity and enforces a sense of blame and shame on the individual level.[19] Zambrana's central argument thus is that debt is a force reinvigorating the coloniality of power.[20] Each time a woman is the victim of domestic violence, or is forcibly displaced as a result of debt, it is "reterritorialization" of the debt onto their bodies.[21] More than explore the material conditions of debt, Godreau-Aubert describes debt as a state of being with affective, physical, and psychological implications for the people who live under it.[22] In my attention to the metaphysics of colonialism, I too am interested in narrating these existential costs of the debt framework.

Debt itself has long been a tool for maintaining structures of inequality, exploitation, and domination in the Caribbean, beginning with the ransom France imposed on Haiti for claiming freedom as a black nation, to the International Monetary Fund's adjustment plans in Jamaica, which had devastating impacts on the cost of food, health, and education.[23] What we have seen time and time again is that debt itself is used by external forces to circumvent any efforts to establish sovereign control locally over one's own land, resources, and future. Puerto Rico is also locked into a colonial position in a postcolonial world. It is captured by this "no place" described by Godreau-Aubert. Aloysha Goldstein makes a similar argument. No matter how exceptional Puerto Rico was created to be within the Cold War context, in the context of debt, it is rather like other Caribbean contexts.

While I am not able to offer a regional analysis of debt, I name Haiti and Jamaica to highlight this work's alignment with anthropological studies of the Caribbean region grappling with the quasi-permanent and unending crisis, impacts of climate change and tourist industry, and "dependency" that is the result of a manufactured and obligatory relationship to US empire. I write this against the exceptionalism that can sometimes plague analyses of Puerto Rico. I trust that from the specificity of this case will emerge many parallels to be explored at a later time in conversation with others.

Yarimar Bonilla and Marisol LeBrón's edited volume *Aftershocks of Disaster: Puerto Rico Before and After the Storm* is another key text on the debt crisis, though its explicit focus is disaster. Borrowing the language of natural disaster from earthquakes, the editors use the concept of aftershocks to define the poststorm moment. For them Hurricane Maria was not a discrete event, but a disaster that triggered more shocks and traumatic impacts that are challenging to differentiate from other events.[24] This was certainly my experience on the ground in the post-Maria moments. I often found myself on brigades organized to attend to physical damages left by the storm, but people we visited preferred to discuss other traumas that had come again to the surface after the storm. Indeed, the trauma provoked by years of neglect and austerity was so profound that even Naomi Klein felt that her work on the shock doctrine was not adequate to express what she witnessed in Puerto Rico. Instead she described the Puerto Rican experience as "shock after shock" in the face of continual structural and systemic violence.[25]

Still, the opening line of the volume troubles me. Drawing from the experience of a hurricane survivor named Isabel who left the island in the immediate aftermath of the storm, they write, "There is no way to win."[26] Despite her safety in the diaspora, she is perpetually depressed and anxious. I understand that Isabel is in an impossible conundrum. She is missing home at the same time she feels she cannot be there. Still, as the opening to the text, these words set a pessimistic tone that is overdetermining and tragic. I hope to complicate the perspective in *Aftershocks* to go beyond the binary framework between winning and losing. How might we restore a sense of possibility by examining how people continue to resist and imagine in the face of trauma? What are the politics of returning and staying in place in the context of aftershocks?

In all the works I have read on the debt crisis, a simple truth emerges: the Puerto Rican people are being forced to pay for a debt not of their own creation. In this formula we are taught to believe there is no way to win. We must pay with everything: our work, our dreams, our bodies, our pensions, and even our mental health. Raquel Salas Rivera makes this point with searing power and criticism with their poetry. He writes, speaking in the voice of those debt collectors: "Tu vida no es suficiente. Tendrás que pagarla con el trabajo de tus hijos y los hijos de tus hijos" (Your life is not sufficient. You will have to pay with your children's work and the children of your children). Reading on, we learn that the author does not have children and is told that in that case the rivers will be the inheritors of their debt.[27] It is both the land and to the future generations who are the successors of this conundrum and of whose life the system will seek further extraction. I went to a reading of Salas Rivera's *Antes que isla es volcán / Before island is volcano* and left destroyed by a grief so vast that I had to fight to not completely disconnect or give up.

To be sure, there is a value to works that can communicate the grief, rage, and pain that comes with witnessing the violences Puerto Rico is forced into through colonial debt and disaster capitalism. But what of those of us living through such violences? Frankly, I believe we need other horizons. Like Ailton Krenak provides in *Ancestral Future*, I rather ground into the movement and power of water itself. The Watu "a body of water on the surface that had the capacity to dive into the Earth in search of deep aquifers and to reshape its path when under attack."[28] May we be willing to go underground as necessary and be ever shifting in our conception of what could be.

I know I am not alone in this longing to affirm possibilities and breaks in the face of a totalizing system. For example, Marisol LeBrón—one of the editors of *Aftershocks*—later wrote *Against Muerto Rico*, drawing on the history of organizers and everyday people ousting Ricardo Rosselló from his place as governor to suggest that protest is a lifegiving response to counter the death spiral of debt.[29] Likewise, Yarimar Bonilla's piece "The Swarm of Disaster" ends where this work begins. She writes: "To think beyond the political disasters of empire we must thus find new tools and epistemic ground from which to not just repair the damages we face, but also re-envision the futures we wish to build."[30] By attending to the ways that people are working from across the archipelago to build alternatives, we get a glimpse of this new ground. By examining the practices of building collective futures in the spaces available to those who stay in Boriké, I hope to reinvigorate a sense of possibility and honor the life that persists beyond disaster.

In many ways the film *Landfall* by Cecilia Aldarondo, which covers the post-Maria moment leading up to the Ricky Renuncia protests, moves in a similar direction to this work.[31] Aldarondo offers a complex and intimate picture of life that affirms the collective trauma, the resilience, and the defiance of the Puerto Rican people. One scene which really stuck with me is of a dinner shared by a group of radical activists from different parts of the left social movement ecosystem. Each complains that they have not had time to process the trauma of the hurricane because there has simply been no time to rest. They commiserate a shared struggle because of the overwhelming burnout they face within the context of disaster capitalism. While I am sympathetic to this feeling, I believe it misses the point.

The system is set up to keep moving, especially in times of crisis when it is likely to accelerate and take advantage of collective suffering to make more profits. As a result, those of us committed to building alternatives must find pockets of time to steal back for our own liberation and we must support each other as we opt out. No system will give us this time. Taking it back will look different everywhere, but at the baseline is the question of how can we care for each other in the conditions we face, even as we dream for another reality.

I am grateful to those tasked with maintaining a view on how debt imprisons us and how the powerful—be they local elite or the United States itself—continue to operate with impunity and no responsibility for the outcome. In this text, I want to invite our attention away from what is broken or what never worked. Indeed, as Mimi Sheller argues, crisis has been imposed on the Caribbean region as a whole, and its dominance as a framework, crisis interferes with our ability to see beyond it.[32] When living in conditions of unending crisis, there is always something else keeping the focus on despair and destruction, be it the slow violence of economic policy or the sudden impact of a hurricane.

As one who works toward sensitizing and healing from these conditions, I find it difficult to wade through these analyses. I find

Adriana Garriga-López's work hugely helpful in this regard. Her work on debt, resurgence, and sovereignty unravels the framework of crisis. Garriga-López offers "decolonial naturecultures" created by feminist art collectives and queer and trans farmers that are "intertwined with but not entirely determined by political economic machinations or biopolitical exigencies" as a way out.[33] These future-oriented forms of organizing require radical shifts in the relationship between people and place can be experienced as liberatory choices. For example, she names "descaling" or "degrowth" as a practice of participating less in traditional markets and living in ways that lower carbon footprint as not only an ethical choice but also one that conditions of extreme shortages require.[34] As a person from the diaspora, I have reckoned with this kind of scaling back and transformation in the ideas of success these decolonial naturecultures demand. Likewise, Garriga-López also questions certain statistical frameworks that are so often repeated that they become dogmatic. The specific example she gives is the statistic that 85 percent of food in Puerto Rico is imported. This data does not account for the food that never enters the market and is shared between friends and neighbors. While there is an important truth revealed through the statistic, when repeated without attending to what is left out by the frame, it conceals more than reveals.

Our words are double-edged swords, describing and creating worlds all at once. There is medicine in repetition. What do we want to repeat? What is necessary? What can we let go of so that another reality may gain a foothold on our patterns, on history, on our pain? I hope to offer insight into the practices, perspectives, and philosophies that are necessary to build collective futures from within this difficult time and beautiful place called Boriké. I am not trying to be positive above all; indeed, there is grief for me too. My hope is that by sensitizing to these truths while refusing to close in the face of them, I help to move us to a someplace beyond debt.

As David Graeber found in his longitudinal study of debt, both religious and legal categories like guilt, sin, and redemption shape even our most basic ideas of right and wrong. Money has always symbolized an obligation, but approaching the problem of debt from the perspective of morality without noting the way that debt has operated as a system of power is too easy.[35] It allows us to avoid stickier questions of how to build a people-centered system that responds with equity and justice to inequality instead of punishment and isolation. In offering both a description of the everyday effects of shouldering the crisis and

examples of ways folks are building alternatives, I hope to draw an outline of this place beyond disaster.

Fred Moten and Steven Harney suggest we abolish debt altogether.
Examining credit as a form of debt that now governs life from the perspective of the "undercommons"—a category they use to designate
marginalized peoples, whether black, indigenous, queer, gender non-
conforming, or poor—they argue that credit has catalyzed the spread of
ruptured relationships. When we are forced to inhabit a system of debt
and credit, we emerge broken. Moten and Harney are convinced that
debt forgiveness does not go far enough. Instead, they advocate for the
destruction of the system itself: an abolition of accounting.

> When we start to talk about our common resources, when we
> talk about what Marx means by wealth—the division of it, the
> accumulation of it, the privatization of it, and the accounting of
> it—all of that shit should be abolished. I mean, you can't count
> how much we owe one another. It's not count-able. It doesn't
> even work that way. Matter of fact, it's so radical that it probably
> destabilizes the very social form or idea of "one another."[36]

The spread of ruptured relationship is particularly stark in the case
of Puerto Rico. Whole families live divided lives, across geographies,
as many grapple with the idea that their homeland is uninhabitable.
Healing these fractures is key to realizing collective liberation. My
own return migration story is steeped in the complexities of indebtedness named by Moten and Harney. Against the economic idea of debt
emerges the idea of radical interdependence. I am forever indebted to
these lands and the antiprivatization movements I witnessed and doc-
umented as a young researcher that transformed my idea of what is
possible. In disability justice circles, debt, dependency, and care are
intimately connected.[37] Rather than refuse the notion that we depend
on each other to survive, these organizers have shown that it is only
when we care and depend on one another that we engage another form
of debt, one that is perhaps more generative than the forms of accounting it usually masks.

My own story of return contributes to the field of US Latinx studies, particularly the scholarship that examines the complex relationship
that exists between home and diaspora. Although this work is not tracking the movement of a group of people but rather speaks to the return
of a single subject, it nevertheless is also committed to healing a false

divide between here and there, while also speaking to the distinct commitments, privileges, and responsibilities each may hold by virtue of their positionalities. Readers interested in this conundrum may refer to appendix A, which includes a list cocreated with my partner Lau Pat R.A. as part of our work to build cross-geographic networks of collaboration between island and diasporic Boricua communities.

The move to Boriké sensitized me in this regard to the hardships one may face in returning to their ancestral lands, a move I have come to think of as rematriation. The rematriation movement itself originated with indigenous women who demanded the return of stolen bones, artifacts, land, culture, and traditions to native peoples.[38] Instead of living in museums or personal collections, rematriation establishes the return of what was stolen as a precursor for indigenous self-determination. Indeed, rematriation is an epistemology for restoring balance to the earth that only becomes possible when cultural knowledge and traditions are returned to the inheritors of this wisdom. I consider the political act of returning to Boriké a kind of rematriation—one where I have returned my body to the land.

The "giving back" inherent in rematriation can occur across mental, spiritual, emotional, and physical terrains. It includes the restoration of right relationships to the earth broadly, away from the patriarchal logics of extraction, violence, and war. In that sense, rematriation signals a return not only to a physical place but also to a way of life. Rematriation is not just about righting past wrong but restoring the sacred in life and transforming our collective future. My dear friend and artist Yasmin Hernandez—AfroBoricua Nuyorican painter, and writer who also returned to Puerto Rico as an adult—calls rematriation a return to the ancestral womb.[39] In returning to our homeland, we are reborn. Closer to the ancestral wisdom that lives in place, a spirit walk begins. Far from easy, this return also means directly witnessing the displacement, disrespect, and harassment commonplace in this archipelago while reaching into deeper streams of wisdom offered by the land. It is a constant balancing act.

Rematriation led me to understand this walk as one of indigenous reclamation. As a Puerto Rican raised in the diaspora, I was fed the myth of Taino extinction.[40] I did not grow up aware of myself as indigenous, although I am gently opening to the truth that I am descendant of this community.[41] As a scholar I learned that the myth of the Vanishing Indian is a powerful heuristic used in all settler colonial contexts to extinguish indigenous claims to the land. I know that many indigenous Boricuas escaped into the mountains, cliffs, and caves at the center of the archipelago, and what we think of as jibaro tradition is where these native inheritances were preserved in plain sight. Yet there is no federal recognition of any native communities in Boriké. In my genealogical research, I find myself led up to the central mountain range, to towns bearing indigenous names of Orocovis and Maricao.

I recognize the immense challenges for anyone wanting to claim an indigenous context in Boriké. I know that from 1898 to 1918, at least sixty Puerto Rican students were sent to Carlisle, the infamous boarding school for indigenous children.[42] Whether these children thought of themselves as Taino or whether they were sent as part of a racial project of assimilation regardless of how they self-identified is up for debate. Still, it begs the question, why should we believe the story of the colonizer over that of the people who have worked for their entire lives to maintain, restore, and revive the traditions and cultures of Taino people?[43]

My own journey of "return" deepened my understanding of the act and practice of decolonization, and thus began my long walk as a person committed to ancestral reclamation. The elders I have the honor to walk with are helping me to reclaim ceremonies, sense of place, and a deeper ability to listen, which I think of as part of an indigenous resurgence movement. In a context where so much was erased, we must be highly cautious and self-aware as we do this work. I believe wanting recognition is a bit of a trap, at least, from a legal perspective but is certainly a powerful motivator. We are, after all, social beings. I consider this work to be deeply shaped by my investment in reclaiming an indigenous context for Boriké.[44]

A final word on lineage. This work is profoundly committed to healing justice, a concept and north star of my activist practice.[45] Created and stewarded by Black and Brown femmes in the US South, healing justice creates mechanisms for wellness and safety that transform conditions of generational trauma and violence.[46] Noting how activists became sick or died before their time because of trauma, stress, and unrest in social movements, healing justice emerged as a path to improve the staying power of organizers by attending to spiritual and physical dimensions of people and communities. Through the multipronged political frameworks of harm reduction, transformative justice, reproductive justice, disability justice, and environmental justice, healing justice is a comprehensive, intersectional approach to liberation.

In Puerto Rico healing justice is inextricably linked to the practice of decolonizing our daily life.

After spending more than ten years working alongside movement changemakers in Puerto Rico and seeing similar patterns of abuse, poor communication, and overwork destroying movements from within, I found a calling. I trusted that answers could emerge from our coming together to grieve, heal, and dream another future. These are precisely the encounters I cocreate and curate now. I hope that these pages offer another opportunity for us to gather the energy to continue building alternative futures in and beyond Boriké.

Methodology of Purpose

At its core, this work is ethnographic. Chapters 2 and 3 are based on qualitative ethnographic fieldwork that I conducted over 2007–11 as part of my dissertation, with periodic follow-up visits through 2015. The interviews for the microhistories in part 2 were conducted between 2016 and 2018. They are based on snowball sampling from the initial period of research I conducted as part of my doctoral studies. The rest of the data is based on my organizing experience, observations, and informal interviews gathered from 2016 into the present.

From this ethnographic foundation, I have strived to craft a creative text centrally concerned with the personal, ethical, and political choices facing us as people living in challenging times. I am inspired by other feminists of color who have long written mixed genre texts to honor the complexity of their position as people critical of their home contexts while deeply loyal to them.[47] As such, in terms of form, *Beyond Disaster* is a crafted blurred-genre ethnographic analysis that weaves history, stories, poetic reflections, and memoir to get at the painful feelings of the status quo while moving into the realm of what might be.

I have done my best to make this work accessible to multiple audiences, so I align my work with the effort of public anthropology whose central concern is to illuminate big social issues of the contemporary moment and encourage dialogue across multiple communities with the explicit goal of fostering social change. Mark Schuller and Gina Ulysse have done much to show the connection between Haiti's struggle for dignity and liberation with the future of life on this planet. I hope to add to this conversation with the specific cases contained within this text on Puerto Rico.[48]

In terms of content this work is most methodologically aligned to the work of US Latinx scholars and artists grappling with decolonial theory. For those unfamiliar, decoloniality is a school of thought aimed at decentering Eurocentric knowledge, hierarchies, and ways of being to make visible other forms of existence on earth that were dismissed, targeted, or repressed through colonialism. Decoloniality was coined by Peruvian sociologist Anibal Quijano and has subsequently been developed by several scholars, artists, and activists. Catherine Walsh's definition is instructive. Decoloniality is "a perspective, stance, and proposition of thought, analysis, sensing, making, doing, feeling, and being that is actional (in the Fanonian sense), praxistical, and continuing."[49] For Walsh, decoloniality is not a mere theoretical position but a practice that unhinges and cracks the system. In other words, decoloniality is a praxis of undoing and affirming plurality where singular dominant views prevent us from seeing otherwise, or beyond the limits of a normative viewpoint.

Thanks to an anonymous reviewer of my work, I learned of Macarena Gómez-Barris's work on social ecologies published the same year as Hurricane Maria hit the island.[50] Her "'femme decolonial method'—the nexus where experience, perception and decolonization meet" echoes my own methodological process.[51] Her attention to the submerged perspectives and the multiplicity of possibilities that exceed the colonial gaze and disciplinary frame within what she calls the "extractive zone" is generative for me. She works across different case studies and geographic contexts to collect stories that would not be read together because they are not from the same nation-state context. Like Gómez-Barris, my work also moves across distinct terrains within a single archipelago and shares her queer commitment to reading against the norm through embodied experience at the edges of perception.

While I certainly see this work contributing to the vast literature emerging on decolonial praxis, I still prefer to use the term decolonization in my day-to-day conversations and organizing. Despite its increasing use outside of realms of higher education, the decolonial is still a niche term that does not easily communicate to people not part of the movement—theoretical or otherwise. But I would be remiss to exclude this work from the decolonial lineage of which it is so clearly a part. As Nelson Maldonado-Torres has described, "decolonial movements tend to approach ideas and change in a way that do not isolate knowledge from action. They combine knowledge, practice, and creative expressions, among other areas in their efforts to change the world."[52] In the same way, as I crafted this text, I found myself needing to move among the realms of theory, practice, and art because our traditional ways of organizing and separating the world need undoing when the horizon is liberation.

Some scholars eschew the use of the term "decolonization" today because of Eve Tuck and K. Wayne Yang's important text that challenged us to only use decolonization when it meant working toward the end of settler colonialism.[53] For them, decolonization is only possible if we are centering the return of lands to original peoples and working toward the removal of settler colonialists from occupied lands. Everything else is social improvement. They caution against the watering down of the decolonization project when it is collapsed into struggles for social justice. Against the metaphorical use of decolonization, the decolonial turn is a powerful way to examine the persistence of colonial structures across contexts and offers a way to examine the partial ruptures from non-Eurocentric modes of being that exceed efforts to erase them.

Still, Puerto Rico is a colony of the United States, so when I situate my writing and activism within the movement for decolonization I am refusing to surrender the terrain. I recognize the complications herein of affirming decolonization as a political project given that colonization as a structure rarely (if ever!) ends when the colonizing force "leaves" and a new sovereign is established. Instead, we have seen that the legal process of decolonization often ends in new people upholding the coloniality of power. To focus on the state solution without healing our relationship to land and our other-than-human kin would be to reproduce the very same structures that keep us imprisoned in the coloniality of power. I think the decolonization of Puerto Rico represents an important symbolic shift in that it offers our people the power to make decisions about the archipelago's future. I say this especially in the moment we are now living in which the fiscal control board overseeing the debt adjustment process was imposed on us by the US government. This board has more power than any of our elected representatives.

My hope is that this work offers us a new vantage point from which to recommit to decolonization as a central intention for all those fighting for collective liberation. In the lens of worldbuilding on the liberation journey, retethering ourselves to the land is a pathway toward undoing coloniality and is essential to decolonizing practice. We can practice feeling good to learn what freedom feels like. We can break with the tendency to replace one sovereign for another. We can affirm a need for all once were oppressed people to be self-determining and commit to the rematriation of land at the same time. That's why in my work as an organizer and healing justice practitioner, I am cultivating our readiness for the possibility of collective liberation.

A Mapping

This book is organized in two parts. Part 1 includes three chapters centering what I call the metaphysics of colonialism. In chapter 1, I offer a series of vignettes which demonstrate in small ways the spiritual, emotional, physical, and psychological dimensions of being forced to shoulder a crisis not of our own making. I center these nonmaterial realms as an effort to bring us into the heart of the system's failings. Chapter 2 explores the student strikes organized against the privatization of the public university system within the official debt crisis period. This is but one example in the general trend toward the foreclosure of the system of education as a whole across the archipelago but one that offers profound insights into the challenge and possibility of direct democratic practice. Chapter 3 turns to the archipelago-wide waves of gentrification. By examining the treatment of the land, we get a sense of the challenges Puerto Ricans face to live in dignity in the current moment. Historically, both land and education have been key battlegrounds for those seeking to colonize as well as those seeking to liberate.

Part 2 examines how Puerto Ricans themselves are building long-term solutions to a failed system from within the fissures of it. I offer three distinct forms as alternatives to the "chapter" style of part 1. Part 2 is structured by a series of microhistories, a prose poem, and a coda. These reflections about the challenges and possibilities of worldbuilding move in unending spirals, deepening with every step, revealing other places to travel and more pieces to heal on the journey toward our collective liberation.

Each microhistory features a different project where Boricuas themselves are actively building alternatives to the system and offering responsive solutions that provide well-being, solidarity, and sustenance in place of suffering and scarcity. The stories in this part are a small sampling of the hundreds of emerging projects, collectives, and organizations building alternatives in Boriké today. These stories represent the places and people who at some point or another welcomed me into their lives and shared their struggles for liberation. The spirals of these movements are not actively tracked here, but many of the microhistories presented here have at least one core member who participated in the 2010 strikes at UPR.

Even though I have since learned of many valuable projects that *move beyond* the colony, I stayed with the first stories that I selected out of a pragmatic desire to finish but also to maintain something of a connection to the resistance threads that were discussed in part 1. These resistances to the continued destruction and sale of our lands to the highest (often, foreign) bidder and the dismantling of public education are important precursors to part 2.

As much as was possible, I developed each of these stories in partnership with core leadership of the featured projects and organizations. The interview structure was informal, but I always provided a few guiding questions ahead of time and then met in person for a conversation in circle. Afterward, I shared the first draft for feedback with participants.

In three microhistories (El Hormiguero, El Llamado, and CEPA) I was not only an interviewer but also an active participant in the space's creation. Ironically, this closeness made my efforts to coordinate an interview process more challenging. Ultimately, I opted to write these microhistories as a reflection based on my experiences. Therefore, they include more discussion of the rough edges where our actions encounter our habits and pain, where exclusion and misunderstanding ensue. My hope is that these self-reflections will make visible the way we can be accountable to our organizing and help us to minimize future harm while building movements where we are all accepted and loved in our imperfection.

In the case of other microhistories where I was not an active participant, I have opted to present the stories as they were told to me. It goes without saying that everywhere we are walking new paths, we will be confronted with the ways we need to change. In other publications I have played with the circulation of "gossip" to highlight internal issues.[54] But this time I felt the important part was to uplift these liberation paths on the terms of the interviewees. I hope that together each style and method provide inspiration for others to engage in their own experiments with liberation. As condensed and brief as they are, I wrote the microhistories inspired by Cherríe Moraga, who wrote, "I will tell you how hungry my body is to know something beyond the colony."[55] Likewise, I offer these microhistories to satisfy our longing for alternatives and as fractal evidence that these alternatives are already material. In turning our attention here, I trace the edges of another country emerging from the ruins. Some of these stories became the focus of public attention as I wrote this manuscript while others escape the mainstream narrative of Boriké operating under the radar. They are movements whose legacies and successes are never accounted for when debt and status are the structuring logics of our future. These microhistories are testimony to the freedom journeys already underway in Boriké.

In lieu of a conclusion, I offer a prose poem to liberation, a poetic rendering of the lessons I learned from my own rematriation journey as well as from the voices featured in the microhistories that are at the heart of part 2. This prose poem is a good place to begin if you are interested in the poetic implications of my work or if you want to go directly into the portal of practicing and reclaiming your sovereignty. The coda offers an "ending" while simultaneously opening to the larger question of how to live with integrity in times of climate change. My sincere hope is that this closing helps to bring into sharp focus the possibilities that lie in the next world we are only just beginning to shape. May it serve as a necessary balm to all people returning home to themselves, to the land, and to each other. May it be an offering to the land and to the people who are building collective futures from within the ruins.

Part 1

Debts: A Metaphysics of Colonialism

Shouldering the Crisis

Puerto Rico is laden with impossible conditions. I made my move here at the crescendo of its latest conundrum—debt—another iteration of a deep-seeded, historic inequality called colonialism. Despite my knowledge of it all, there was an inevitable shock that came with living and working from within the conditions I had for so long studied from afar.

I get that folks want to audit the debt. Really, I do. It's a process that the government has outright rejected. Governor Garcia Padilla, who declared the debt unpayable, dragged his feet at the idea of appointing members to the commission. Then, when Ricky Rosselló was governor, he eliminated the commission altogether. La Frente Ciudadano para la Auditoria de la Deuda formed in the aftermath. Some members were part of the original government initiative, taking matters into their own hands. La Frente believes that having the hard facts about the public debt would ensure a just process of accounting. If the culprits could be verified in an auditory process, the thinking goes, we could declare some parts of the debt illegitimate and be released from some of these obligations, especially the debt that exceeds the maturation limits set out by the island's constitution.

La Frente is not alone in challenging the debt. Puerto Rico's Centro de Periodismo Investigativo (Center for Investigative Journalism) has long been on board, as well as a whole diverse group of grassroots community organizations and political groups. I have participated in gatherings with organizers from both US-based and archipelago-based groups battling against the debt. But to my mind, auditing doesn't go deep enough into the heart of the problem. To call the debt illegitimate by invoking the island's constitutional limits is problematic to say the least. Touted by some as the "end" of the colonial relationship, the island's constitution was only democratically "approved" once it had been modified by members of the US Congress—making it more palatable to our colonizers. The constitution isn't all that much of a

25

protection anyway since Article 6, Section 8, establishes that in times of financial hardship, the government's priority must be to pay its debt.

If we are to move beyond the logic of debt to build a collective future based on responsibility, we need a new way of reckoning. To begin this unraveling of the unsustainable logic of debt and credit, I offer a series of brief vignettes combining autoethnography, storytelling, and poetic reflections that get at the underbelly of debt(s). If you, dear reader, are not yourself Puerto Rican, I ask that you listen first as a gesture of solidarity. For to know what others carry is the first step in sharing the load. If you are Puerto Rican, I hope that these vignettes help you feel seen and reflect the struggles you have faced to stay in (or leave) your ancestral lands.

Nonessential Services

Life in debt means a whole host of your necessities are not covered.
They are superfluous. Expendable. Take it or leave it. Unnecessary. Secondary to payment.
Not food water shelter or even home family community health(care) education dignity.
Not you.
Not me.
Not anything but money. But you can't eat money. You can't drink money. You can't build another planet earth with money.

> But suffering?
> Now, that's essential.

Up until a certain point, most of us forget about the debt. It is hidden by the numbness of trying to make it in amerikkka's oldest colony. We are bracing for the next thing. You need a lot of coping mechanisms when dealing with power outages, water rationing—not because there's a drought, but because the reservoirs haven't been cleaned in years—or extreme heat waves.
Plus, there's buses that don't come. Doctor visits that take all day.
I'm amazed when I make it through another day.

> Survival is no antidote,
> but it sure does feel like the amnesia for debt.

The Lie of the Century

I can't tell you how many times I have been told that there's no money. We have become so used to this lie that we begin from a point of lack in every interaction. Even when I am negotiating a gig with a foundation with more than a $1 billion budget, I get told this lie. "It's just Melissa, listen. The legal team always requires we do a comparison with rates of other people working in Puerto Rico and yours are just way out of range." I feel myself boil with rage. I resist the urge to scream and assert, "Look, folks are used to working for less than they deserve. It doesn't make it right." It's hard to keep decorum in these long-winded meetings, knowing that my would-be clients are making a very comfortable salary while I am worried about how I will pay rent if I don't get the job. I make some cuts to try and land the contract while I wonder, why do those who have, refuse to consider a real redistribution plan? Why are those on the receiving end of budgetary cuts not the same people making the decisions about what to cut? I get the job, but am not paid for four months. "Thank you for your patience on this Melissa. I wish I could do more, but my hands are tied." The lies of bureaucracy are padded by comfortable complicity.

Se acabaron las Promesas (*Promises are over*)

Word spread that Puerto Rico's Commerce Department was going to host a conference to explore the potential market "opportunities" two months after PROMESA (Puerto Rico Oversight, Management, and Economic Stability Act) was passed. Bankers, corporate executives, and government officials were invited to strategize and socialize. A group formed to block the conference from happening. They plastered the city with the phrase "Se acabaron las Promesas." On the day of the conference, in the early morning, busloads of protestors showed up and blocked the front of the hotel where the event was to be held. They spilled over from sidewalks into the street, blocking the road and the bridge. It was one of those vital moments of collective action when we fight and win. Even the police were forced to turn away. Only the conference attendees who were staying on site were able to attend; the vast majority were kept from networking our future away.

I was preparing to return and listened to the accounts via phone. I cried a mix of joy and frustration. The energy was palpable across miles of ocean. Vibrant and fierce, my diaspora blues melted away. This was a clear NO to the uninhabitable future that the fiscal board represented. Some days we forget how powerful we are. But not today.

Uneven Development

Relief workers hired by FEMA to support recovery efforts have their pick of hotels after Hurricane Maria. A locally based gringa who works for them, despite her moral concerns, tells me that the out-of-town workers are given more than $300 per night for housing, almost as much as we pay a month for rent. All the fanciest hotels are booked for months in advance.[1] Many choose to stay at the boutique hotel El Convento in Old San Juan, where wine and cheese is served daily even though most islanders are living without electricity. True to its origins as a Carmelite convent, the building hosts spirits and present-day colonial practice. I hope the ghosts of those cloistered nuns haunt them into eternity.

Concierge Class

If we stay on the surface of Puerto Rico's debt, we miss the professional Boricuas facilitating the sale of our island archipelago. We call these self-appointed intermediaries the concierge class. Be they bad translators, real estate brokers, accountants, or attorneys, these *amigos* are willing to sell anything for a fee. Many offer personalized service, extra perks like brown faces that legitimize a purchase. Carmen Marcano, Ivonne Marie Rodriguez, and Luis Lomba have been working specifically with tax-haven beneficiaries. They are a part of an invisible concierge class and have been particularly successful in attracting hundreds of clients. But I see the concierge class everywhere: attending auctions, leaving voice messages to their friends as we wait on food truck lines, and even meeting one when my partner was evicted. They are a threat to the future of our life on this land. I try to not let hate seep into my veins. Some days it is easier than others.

Congressional Listening Session on Puerto Rican Issues

On Friday March 15, 2019, the House Committee on Natural Resources held a "listening session" in Puerto Rico's Roberto Clemente Coliseum. I registered the day before, mainly as a favor to a friend who works in Washington, DC. I had low expectations; at this point, the US Congress is still only "listening" and identifying issues? But I was surprised to receive a notification that I could only be added to a waitlist for admittance on-site. The coliseum has capacity for nine thousand people. I quickly realized upon arrival that the notification was an effort to turn people away. There were plenty of empty seats in the space. The congressional members sat on a stage, elevated above us—a symbol impossible to ignore. From the floor folks from all walks of life took their three-minute turns at the podium to present the issues. I could hear the devastation in some voices while others sounded well-polished.

I was not ready for facing the truth of the statehood movement. Every day the statehood movement grows, another irony of life in America's oldest colony. I was literally shoved out of the way by a block of state-hooders as they came in forcing their way to the front of the line. They pushed and chanted, "Estadidad, Estadidad!" (Statehood!)

Statehooders have appropriated the term "decolonization" for their movement, sanitizing it of its radical possibility. In their logic, only full incorporation as a state of the union is the equivalent to freedom. They barely engaged during the session save for the moments they screamed to cheer on another statehooder or when they booed then mayor of San Juan, Carmen Yulin. She stopped midspeech to apologize to the board for her people's behavior.

Water Is Life

While most of the news cycle focuses on the increase in electricity costs since the privatization of the energy grid by LUMA Energy, no one talks about the water bills. I'm not exactly sure how long it has been a problem, but it's everywhere. First in our apartment in Puerta de Tierra (PDT), the bills were so high, we had to challenge them month after month. My partner began to investigate only to discover that the meter did not work and hadn't worked for years. The estimated bill was for upward of $300 a month, in an apartment with no appliances, only two ecologically conscious residents. At the office of Acueductos y Acantarillados (Aqueducts and Sewers Authority) Lau was told that the factory manufacturing the meters closed and the Authority was relying on shipments to replace the faulty meters. Thousands were in the same situation, and the representative of the water company doubted the situation would be rectified anytime soon. Later, in another apartment in Río Piedras, bills were extremely high without reason. Still, the debt is placed on the individual to submit a claim monthly. If you don't, the debt is uncontestable. If you send in a claim and receive a letter "verifying the legitimacy" of the previous bill and fail to respond within ten days, the debt is uncontestable. Amid everything else, it adds a weight, a worry that feels bottomless. How can you contest a whole system every day with so little energy? You rather just not even deal with it. You'd rather just put it away and forget about it. After all, it's not your debt.

But that part gets lost because you are facing a system with their bureaucracy and their massive teams and their unlimited time. You are facing the possibility that you will never have access to water again and your access to an everyday service will be cut off. Rather than feel like the debt is illegitimate, like these people are crazy, even the most radical of us can feel guilt, shame, or even blame. The judge inside gets activated and we search for fault. Isolated from our springs and rivers, we forget the water flowing through PVC pipes unencumbered by the logics of capital. Life prevails if we can align with the flow.

Vieques

I traveled to Vieques on a small airplane—a luxury I usually cannot afford—when I was hired in 2019 by a nonprofit based in Washington, DC, to facilitate story circles on the island. The price to fly at that time was close to $150 per person for a twenty-minute flight in a small ten-person airplane while the ferry only costs $3 per person. Of course, the ferry can take anywhere from two hours to all day if there are delays due to maintenance issues, fuel shortages, or out-of-commission boats. I can almost guarantee that there are delays today. There were delays yesterday and likely tomorrow. On the plane, a white woman from Georgia excitedly tells us about her new land purchase in Vieques. She got it for way under asking price, she brags, by offering cash. She got the money by taking out a second mortgage on her home and was marveling at what a great deal it was. She was excited to build a vacation home of her dreams. I wondered whether the previous owner was themselves a Viequenese and would be forced like the four thousand others to leave their island for other lands.

Steal Your Property

When I first arrived in Puerto Rico in 2016, my friends and family encouraged me to buy. Take advantage of the crisis, they said. I innocently dreamed that I could buy something with the little savings I had accrued over the few years while I was working as a postdoc and visiting professor. When I attended an auction, I told myself that I was working to do something good for my community and it didn't matter if I acquired it in this way. "Ends justify the means," as the saying goes. The auction was being performed by a group from the Deep South named John Dixon & Associates. Dixon & Associates is a private equity fund that specializes in the Caribbean and Latin America. Its local partners were Aurora Properties and Christiansen Commercial. Both are real estate firms that have been facilitating purchase en masse of property by foreign investors in Puerto Rico. There were no more than twenty bidders in the room, about equally divided between Puerto Ricans and gringos. They ranged from a middle-aged couple, a mother-daughter duo, a mixed-race couple who only spoke English, the crew of youngish men in jeans and t-shirts, to older retired white (Puerto Rican) men with balding heads and reading glasses and khaki pants. The bidding itself was intense. Combined with the southern cadence and the buzzing, fast paced rhythmic sounds of the bidding, it was hard to stay present. The sounds triggered in me the memory of racism and theft of another kind. During the bidding, John Dixon nonchalantly spoke a future into existence: "Alright y'all. Don't be shy. And if you were wondering, it IS gonna sell . . . there IS no tomorrow . . . this market IS gonna turn." He bragged he would be going to Piñones afterward for a cold *medalla* (beer) and *alcapurria* (fritter made of green bananas and taro root) with his amigo Juan. I lasted only through the first thirteen sales, until the nausea overtook me, and I walked out feeling small. In 2023 the city of Vieques held an open auction on several pieces of land, all out of reach for the vast majority of Viequeneses. A group of local people protested it and blocked the sale, for now.

State of Emergency

Femicides and transfemicides are commonplace occurrences in Puerto Rico. Thanks to the work of key feminist organizations like La Colectiva Feminista en Construcción and Proyecto Matria, we know that one woman or girl is murdered every seven days. Once a week someone we love won't be coming home. A lot of folks will have you believe that's because of the stresses associated with the unending crisis, but few will speak directly to the links between this violence and the conservative and powerful religious right in Puerto Rico. Finally, after a twenty-nine-year-old nurse named Angie Noemi González was murdered at the hands of her ex, who threw her body into a ditch after he strangled her to death, Governor Pedro Pierluisi declared a state of emergency. Many civil organizations celebrated this win. It felt like a power play to me, since during his campaign for governor Pierluisi was accused of sexual harassment by his physical trainer. The state of emergency had its benefits because it meant more resources would be allocated to "combat" gender-based violence and a special representative to be appointed to oversee this work. But I doubt we would agree on what we need to combat. Neither the police data nor the Registry of Vital Statistics include entries for transgender people. When Alexa Negrón Luciano was murdered in 2019—a black, homeless, trans artist—nothing happened. She was interviewed by police after using a women's bathroom in McDonalds in Toa Baja. Less than twelve hours later, she was shot multiple times and her body was left on the side of the road. Two videos went viral. One was the video taken by appalled clients who claimed she was a man in the woman's bathroom using a mirror to spy on "real" women. The second was a video of her being murdered amid taunting and gunshots. The police interviewed four teens about the incident but never arrested anyone. Alexa carried a broken rearview mirror everywhere to see who was behind her. Those of us awake to the contradictions have nothing left to do but look at ourselves in the mirror and see this country for what it has become.

Boquetes (*Gaps*)

After Hurricane Maria I learned firsthand that official stories miss the depth of the scale of inconsistent access to electricity in a dramatic way. I lived in Puerta de Tierra, very close to the capitol building, which shone in multicolor irony through the darkness of our neighborhood from the very first days post-Maria. In less than two months, electricity was restored to the front of the building—a privilege considering that more than 80 percent of islanders lived without electrical power for more than four months after the storm—but we continued to live in the dark for two additional months because the building had two electricity connections and only one of them was restored. Each evening I walked up the well-lit staircase to the dark apartment wondering when we'd ever get service. Ultimately, it was a personal connection that got us back online. My neighbor was riding her bike in Santurce when she ran into a friend who had moved to New York. He was working for Con

Edison and she explained the situation. He and his crew agreed to follow her back to our apartment, a large truck trailing her as she led them on her bike to our building. When my partner and neighbor helped the workers locate the connection, they took one look at the frayed cable and said they simply thought it was a remainder of a previous connection, so old it looked like it came from "Noah's Ark." Workers from other regions unfamiliar with the precarious conditions of our electricity grid missed many connections in this way. Still, they were paid triple what a worker with the electrical company on the island would have earned. We inhabit these gaps, unperceived by the official numbers and news stories, eager to announce victory in a reconstruction process bent on "restoring" order without making a single change to the way our electricity grid is wired.

The gaps continue to widen along with the continuing drama of the privatization of Puerto Rico's electric grid. On June 1, 2021, LUMA Energy took over the island's electricity system and since then there have been regular and widespread outages. LUMA is made up of three businesses: ATCO, a Canadian utility and construction company; Quanta Services, a US company focusing on building infrastructure; and IEM, a company specializing in the management of federal funds. LUMA itself was only formally registered as a corporation in Puerto Rico in January 2020. Their contract was negotiated behind closed doors and only announced after it had been finalized. LUMA was supported by la junta, even as Puerto Rican legislators expressed concerns. LUMA's contract stipulates they will not be held liable in the event of a large-scale collapse of Puerto Rico's power grid across a whole range of possible scenarios including natural disaster. If another hurricane like Hurricane Maria leaves the island in the dark, they will likely just walk away. In the meantime, outages continue. Our bills have already increased seven-fold, and la junta's proposed agreement with bondholders includes bill increases of up to 50 percent over forty years, directly affecting the pockets of our families, and in the case of the poorest could represent up to 40 percent of their income.

Heat Waves

"You are worth so more than your productivity" has got to be my favorite anticapitalist love note.[2] I've become so practiced in the patterns of creating, producing, and "doing" that I've learned to associate productivity with who I am. The challenge of unlearning this association takes on a new meaning in the extended heat waves of 2023. For more than six months, we faced regular heat indexes above 108 degrees across the coastline and in major cities all over the archipelago. During this time, we are warned to stay inside for most of the workday, drink lots of liquids, and avoid exerting ourselves. I regularly find my thinking is sluggish at best, cloudy at worst. In the haze, I try to press on. One day, I stop to clean the kitchen only to be covered in sweat within ten minutes. I stand up too quickly and am overcome with dizziness. I live without air conditioning so I sit down in front of the fan after dousing myself in water and peppermint oil for a brief respite. On most nights, I wake up drenched in sweat, take a cold shower, and go back to the bed dripping wet as I try and find a window into sleep. The gift, if any, that the heat offers is clarity that the unstoppable rhythm that is capitalism is unsustainable. I feel the waves of grief, anger, and fear at what will happen if we don't find a way to stop under these conditions. On days I am really tapped into the truth that I am more than what I do, I steal back my time in the form of morning swims, canceled meetings, and afternoon naps. I recognize this is a privilege in deep waves of sadness.

Our Dead

The government death tolls after Hurricane Maria blatantly denied the enormity of the impact of the storm. The official death toll topped out at sixty-four but the accepted number internationally is closer to five thousand (4,645 to be exact).[3] Interruption in medical care due to electricity outage was the primary cause of increased deaths after the storm. People who were in long-term stays at hospitals or in supported living facilities were discharged. Others who depended on regular maintenance procedures like dialysis also died. Then there were those who could not withstand the sight of so much destruction and died from shocks in the form of heart attacks and strokes. The signs of a weight too heavy for their bodies to bear. Others committed suicide. There were other-than-human kin such as pigeons and parrots in corners and alleyways who hadn't survived the winds. The eldest standing people were strewn about on the roads and sidewalks with their roots upwards. Then there were the bees who wandered into our city apartment, lost and confused for the first couple weeks. With nothing left to pollinate they were drawn in by sweet smells, like sweet plantains in coconut oil, or black coffee and brown sugar.

Hoarding

How could a people be so tied to scarcity when they have so much? Because we are looking elsewhere. Because we are being robbed. In the post-Maria moments, relief monies were being funneled to US corporations and friends of friends in our government who claimed they could "help" immediately after the storm. And three years later, this lie continued to reveal itself when a security guard person accidentally discovered supplies in a warehouse full of unused and mostly expired supplies, including food, water, cots, and baby formula that were hoarded by the Puerto Rican government. Outside, people were living in their cars, in municipal and military encampments and parks because earthquake swarms had pushed them out of their homes. Although the island's director of the Office of Emergency Management, Carlos Acevedo, was fired for the revelation, the government tried to avoid responsibility by slowing the process of reporting about the storage and were unwilling to produce names of those involved. The state's story changed multiple times, and the truth kept disappearing.[4] I wonder how many dollars disappeared in the name of recovery. What could that money have supported, had it been in the hands of those who understood the meaning of energy exchange, medicine, and freedom? The money never trickles down. And so, we see what is lost, and it marks us. Some of us hold on for too long, due to a lack of capacity or because we don't know where to put something. But it's time we stop worshiping money and remember it is a resource among many. We could put it into circulation, with a change of perspective and a little creativity.

The Only Thing You Can Decolonize Is Yourself

We begin "looting" abandoned properties' fruit trees and joke we should start a social media campaign #okupatucosecha (occupy your harvest). We load up several pounds of ripe, fallen mangoes into milk crates with our solidarity visitor, Ester Aviles, and make jam so sweet it doesn't need sugar. When we manage to steal joyous moments like this from the drudgery of everyday, our physical and emotional energies are transformed. There is a certain satisfaction anytime I can tune out the social and economic dramas and tune into this land Boriké. It's a reminder that there's not only sacrifice for those who stay. We know there's value here. This is, after all, still paradise. Forgotten fruit trees and trade winds covered in concrete and yet, still teeming with life. The land asks me to put roots down and align. Each time I eat something that I harvest, I am reminded of your power, which is also my power and is also, our power. Remembering that is the truth path home.

School Closures and
Student Strikes

Schools are one of the major targets in the debt crisis. Declining numbers of students, and even well-paid teachers can be used as justification for closing schools despite the very clear value schools hold for a society. At their best, schools can foster critical thinking and a sense of responsibility for the future of a country. Given the massive cuts to all forms of public education on the archipelago authorized by la junta, the limited work opportunities which await youth upon graduation from higher education and a long legacy of radical organizing among teachers and students alike, it's no surprise the University of Puerto Rico (UPR) is on the frontlines of organizing efforts to protect accessible public education.[1] In the face of austerity, student organizers have waged impressive battles to protect university autonomy from privatization at the hands of both insular and federal government forces.[2]

Truth be told, students worldwide are facing the reality that finishing a four-year college program is no guarantee of future employment. In Puerto Rico, job prospects are increasingly limited to tourism and low-paying jobs in the service sector independent of the level of education a person may have. Many youth have found themselves on "standby" as they put their futures on hold while they search for ways to survive.[3] For student organizers, building another world was not mere rhetoric used in the movement, but it also represented a very urgent need to make a future for themselves and the country itself.

In this chapter I discuss the three strikes at UPR organized during the period of the debt crisis: 2006–17. I came to know this struggle intimately through the 2010 student strikes at UPR, as I was in Boriké conducting field research and spent a great deal of time there. Although I was little more than a witness at the time, the system wide mobilization had a long-term impact on me. I shifted the direction of my research and life, becoming part of my inspiration to return to Puerto Rico in 2016.

All three mobilizations that occurred between 2006 and 2017 followed the principles of participatory democracy. Consequently, their efforts were shaped by a commitment to radical inclusion in the process. Each of the mobilizations sought to foster autonomy and a lived sense of interdependence across distinct collectives within their mobilizations. In other words, students' fight also was an effort to create an alternative to the dominant currents of disaster capitalism, corruption, and police repression. Their lessons are a vital lifeline to anyone interested in building collective futures from a crumbling system.

Tuition Hikes and Privatization

The first strike that emerged during the "debt period" of Puerto Rican history was organized in 2005, one year before the budget crisis was declared. The strike was known by the acronym for the committee who led it—CUCA (Comité Universitario Contra el Alza, or University Committee Against the Rise). CUCA formed to protest a proposed 33 percent tuition hike by the administration at the time. Students were also protesting the construction of Plaza Universitaria (university plaza), a complex of buildings located across the street from the flagship campus in Río Piedras that would be home mainly to private businesses and a few administrative offices. Organizers were opposed because they understood it to be part of a larger plan to invite private industry into the public institution.

The mobilization lasted twenty-nine days and was marked by constant division. This was because the elected student governance body continued to operate during the strike and was opposed to the grassroots-organized collective CUCA. Student council took any opportunity to block interventions of CUCA organizers and actively aligned with the administration itself. This division created a picture of a confused and embattled student body in the public eye.

Despite the fraught public portrait of the strike, CUCA was born as an alternative structure to the bureaucratic and exclusive methods with which the student council operated. The premise behind CUCA was that each student had a right to speak and vote. According to interviews with student leader and sage organizer, Giovanni Roberto Cáez, this strike was a "practice session" for the systemwide mobilization that was to come five years later. Indeed, many of the key elements of the 2010 strike already existed in seed form during CUCA. For example, there was a national movement forming in opposition to the tuition hike. Although the 2005 strike was popularly understood as a strike of the Río Piedras campus, all eleven campuses protested the tuition hike. Four other campuses joined in CUCA's declaration for a general strike to oppose the measure.

Discursively and organizationally, CUCA was invested in direct democracy. In the discourse of the strike, the organizers questioned the inevitability of budgetary cuts and raising costs of everyday life that all politicians accepted as inevitable. In writings about the CUCA strike Giovanni Roberto reflected that the strikers held both mainstream political parties—PNP (New Progressive Party or Partido Nuevo Progresista, in Spanish and PPD, or the Popular Democratic Party and Partido Popular Democrático in Spanish) responsible for the crisis by approving austerity measures.[4] By making clear that not only statehooders (PNPs) but also the status quo party (PPD) has supported changes that were detrimental to life as we know it on the island, these organizers moved beyond the polarizing politics played in the electoral sphere in their discourse. They noted that both parties used crisis as an excuse to push through cuts in services. If debt and crisis were seen as acceptable reasons to raise the cost of living, there would be no future for the youth.

The ability to show the parallels between the issues faced by the island population overall and what was happening at the institution was important for expanding the movement. Even though projected changes would significantly affect the accessibility of the institution, strikers were derided in public forums as well as within the student body and were unable to unify sectors of the university significantly. Many people believed that CUCA was an invention of a minority group, not a participatory democratic structure in formation.

Organizationally too, CUCA shifted its method. For the first time in history, strikers developed a general coordinating committee. This body represented the students in negotiations with administrators and was connected to a series of grassroots committees across the student body. Organizers at the Río Piedras campus started to dialogue with students at other campuses within the public institution since tuition hikes affected them all, creating a sense of common struggle. They were not only concerned with cuts to already existing curricular offerings; they saw the root cause went beyond the university and understood that all public sectors were facing a shared danger. Radical as it was, the central coordinating committee had not developed a protocol for dialoguing with its base and consequently, it did not have a clear path for making decisions collectively, making them susceptible to pressure from university administrators.

When CUCA organizers signed an agreement with the administration without consulting the larger student body of strikers, it caused much strife. Voting on these agreements in the early hours of the morning without discussing it with the larger student body was largely understood to be the movement's biggest downfall. By not including other members of the mobilization in this process of approving the negotiated agreement, they went against the core principles of participatory democracy. The result was a feeling of great loss, exclusion, and defeat. All student strikers managed to gain was an extension for paying the tuition hike. Even that was not for everyone; it would be awarded on a case-to-case basis. The tuition hike was imposed as planned and building of Plaza Universitaria was completed.

A Magical Confluence: *La huelga creativa* (The creative strike)

Many of the difficulties faced by strikers during CUCA served as the groundwork to make for one of the most successful student protests in history. The catalyst was a new policy instituted by the Board of Trustees of the UPR system in 2009, called Certification 98. It eliminated "double" eligibility for tuition waivers based on need and merit. In other words, Certification 98 made students choose between need or merit-based tuition waivers. They could no longer receive both the Federal Pell Grant awarded based on the income level of their parents or tuition waivers based on their merit as an athlete or high-achieving student. Organizers named this act "no double dipping," a tongue-in-cheek way to poke fun at this classist move.

Protests to Certification 98 brought together a vastly diverse group of students and included new activists as well as those who were more seasoned, such as the organizers of leftist groups like International Socialist Organization (Organization Socialista Internacional [OSI]). These older activists contributed a deep critique of class and capital to the larger movement analysis. Newcomers included athletes and high-ranking students and vast numbers by students from both humanities and arts departments who enlivened the mobilization with creativity and performance arts.

A popular figure of this strike was the "dead university," which represented what the public system would become under the proposed austerity measures. Lawyers in training, thought to be among the most conservative of the entire student body, also joined the mobilization and played a key role in securing an injunction to protect the occupation of the campus itself in the first days. It was evident to everyone that this was no minority group.

When the 2010 strike began as a forty-eight-hour walk out on April 21 at the Río Piedras campus, organizers had spent nearly two semesters building power with others and developing a shared analysis. Students organized walkouts, camping trips, assemblies, and a host of other techniques to create a robust dialogue across campus.[5] Discussions about the proposed changes occurred across multiple autonomous sectors, loosely organized as action committees.

Action committees were mass organizing bodies open to any student. Eventually, they would evolve into *comités de base* (grassroots committees) loosely organized by department (social sciences, arts, humanities, natural sciences, law), home to distinct communities that focused on the issues most relevant to their divisions. These committees later would become encampments, each their own subcultural home located across the campus with their own decision-making power and autonomy within the mobilization. These groupings were joined by committees that already existed before the strike including: Comité Contra la Homofobia y el Discrimen (the Committee Against Homophobia and Discrimination, or CCHD) and Comité de Estudiantes en Defensa de la Educación Pública (the Committee in Defense of Public Education, or CEDEP). The strikers also elected a group to negotiate with the institution's Board of Trustees (National Negotiating Committee).

The strike quickly spread across all the eleven campuses of the public university system. It was the first systemwide strike in the institution's more than one-hundred-year history and lasted for sixty-three days. It would take a book onto itself to write about what happened in those sixty plus days of struggle. The real sense of possibility, something you could feel palpably at times, in the months of rain and stagnation, intermingling with the exhaustion and frustration, and sometimes even disillusionment as when internal battles over tactics, treatment of the university of property and the question of "who" had ultimate power were at the fore. All these issues brought into sharp clarity the challenges and possibilities of direct democratic practice.

The explicit target of the 2010 strike was the Board of Trustees, but the demands were expansive. In addition to the repealing of Certification 98, students demanded a guarantee that the university system would not be privatized through the public-private partnerships (P3s) being formed at the government level. It also included a moratorium on tuition hikes.[6] Lastly, students demanded that the university find alternatives to reduce the deficit that did not place the responsibility on already burdened students.

Having learned from the CUCA strike, the organizers created a student coordinating committee made up of representatives from each of the smaller grassroots committees. Their role was to make sure that there was a process through which everyone could be involved in decision making. Prior to the strike, the student coordinating committee's role was to convene mass assemblies that all committees participated in. It was only at these sessions that decision-making for the whole movement took place, although each group met on their own and got into alignment on certain issues before attending plenaries.

Individual committees convened regularly to develop proposals and raise concerns to present during the daily plenary sessions of the entire student body. When the strike started to spread beyond the Río Piedras campus to the other campuses, they also modified their negotiating committee's shape to fit the national context. A new series of assemblies were convened, and the National Negotiating Committee was formed. The National Negotiating Committee had more members from the Río Piedras campus since they had the most experience, but each campus had the same number of votes. Negotiations were coordinated while up-to-the minute briefings and report-backs were issued to the collective. Decisions were made only after the collective had a chance to deliberately discuss and approve positions.

The early injunction secured by strikers from the law school not only kept police and school officials off campus, but it also forced the Board of Trustees to enter a negotiating process after their efforts to ignore, or "wait out" the student mobilization had failed to end the conflict. The court—already involved in the process by way of injunction—ordered the school administrators enter a mediation with the student's national negotiating committee and assigned a retired judge to the case. On June 16, 2010, after five days of court-mandated mediation, students won. The Board of Trustees voted nine to four in favor of entering an agreement with the students, agreeing to eliminate Certification 98, waive the proposed tuition increase, and not suspend key leaders.

Amid the negotiations, students learned that the administration planned to mandate a new $800 fee to the enrollment costs the following semester, an action that was projected to leave ten thousand students unable to continue their studies. Key leaders were targeted by the administration—Adriana Mulero Claudio, Ian Camilo Cintrón Moya, Giovanni Cáez, and Waldemiro Velez Soto—and received notice of expulsion. They were not allowed to return to campus to continue their studies. This surprise turn of events shaped the end of the protest deeply for those already disillusioned and exhausted.

When the 2010 strike culminated at the first national convening of all campuses gathered to approve the agreements that were negotiated by National Negotiating Committee and the Board of Trustees, the student body unilaterally approved a "preventative strike" for the next semester were the "special fee" imposed. Perhaps they were trying to regain a sense of control. But the move forced them into another mobilization the following semester, distinct in almost every way.

First, the university was occupied by private security—making any sense of another country protected from the strictures and repression of our current world—impossible to contain. The gates of the university were removed in some places to strategically prevent strikers from taking physical control of the campus and forcing another closure of the institution. The battle over strategy especially in terms of how to respond to the violent repression authorized by the administration created immense strife from within. Student participation in the action declined significantly. In the first strike, numbers were closer to two thousand at the peak of the action. The second strike had, on average, about three hundred students involved.

One of the correspondents and cofounders of Radio Huelga (Strike Radio), Ricardo, referenced this closure, describing it as a streamlining of perspectives brought about by a loss of diversity. "We were basically the same people, we already had gone through a whole process together, so we'd come to see things in a similar way, but we lost some of that flexibility that was so useful in the first strike." Given the size and the pressures that the strikers were facing, it's no surprise that this mobilization could not achieve what student-organizers had in 2010. In addition, there was really no time to process the internal issues which had emerged and develop a new strategy. The issue of roles and "right" behavior was left unresolved and by the end of the strike, many had conflicting feelings about the mobilization itself. Serious divisions surfaced. There were internal issues related to gender violence, tactics, and a changing notion of the role of the "charismatic" leader that were left unresolved at the end of the last strike. Instead of being given time to heal and regroup, the organizers were thrown into battle again. Others graduated. Those who returned found themselves facing exhaustion, unemployment, and a tuition fee that they simply could not pay.

Despite its challenges, the creative strike was a beautiful exercise in building collective power. The 2010–11 movement shifted toward building leaderful movements even as organizers struggled to shed the dynamics which led to the centering and uplifting of some over others. It didn't achieve everything, but it was a moment of radical possibility impossible to erase from the memories and bodies of those who lived it together. It promoted a sense of direct responsibility, interdependence, and, at times, joy.

La gran huelga (The great strike)

Things went quiet for more than five years at the UPR until 2017 when a new movement emerged. On March 28, 2017, students organized a weeklong strike followed by an indefinite strike that lasted for about two months and included mobilizations at seven of the eleven campuses. Strikers explicitly understood their mobilization as a continuation of the concerns that drove the 2010 strike. The biggest question for them was to try and answer the question that their predecessors could not: how could they link their mobilization with the issues facing the island as whole? La gran huelga was organized in a response to a budget cut of $450 million to the public university system, proposed by la junta.

For the first time in history, the student mobilization's target was not within the university system but was the central government of Puerto Rico. Students demanded that the government repeal Law 66—a law that temporarily froze transfers from the general fund—and restore funds taken from the university. They demanded that the treasury department stop making debt payments until it could be audited. They also demanded that the government revise the formula by which the UPR's budget was determined. Finally, in a bold and radical move, they demanded that the government hold a constitutional referendum and change the priority of putting debt before investing in the future of the archipelago. Organizers knew that all the cuts they faced at the UPR began with the constitution which stated that all debts must be paid before funding public services.

As in 2010, students organized for about a year, including the little discussed five-day stoppage organized in 2016, prior to the strike. Their strategies included Twitter flurries, sign-making gatherings before protests, and even showing up to classes to give brief presentations on their analysis of the crisis. The cross-sector participation in the protests made this protest distinct. Even professors were frightened by the cuts proposed by the university, and they openly spoke out in classes, shifting the tides in the historically conservative divisions of science and business administration. Students also developed informational videos for circulation on the internet that drew the connections between the debt and the conditions they were facing at the university.

Their early efforts led to extremely high levels of participation in the process. When the strike was approved on April 5, 2017, every single amphitheater at the Río Piedras campus was filled. About two thousand students, or nearly 25 percent of the entire student body voted in favor of the strike. Estimates suggest that around four thousand to five thousand students were part of the mobilization overall, more than double the numbers of participants in the 2010 strike. This increase demonstrated a growth into previously unorganized communities within the student body. Even within the leadership, there were students who had no previous organizing experience.

Instead of staying within the gates as prior mobilizations had done, the new student-organizers took their protest directly to the source of the conflict and blocked the entrance to El Departamento de Hacienda (the government's treasury department) until Undersecretary Juan Flores Galarza agreed to sit down and negotiate with the students. While little in the way of formal changes may have come from this meeting, it demonstrated student bravery. They not only shifted the discourse, but the locus of the battle for public education. Their action made visible the way that spending practices of the government had limited the viability of public education.

Student organizers continued to mobilize outside the campus. Their task, according to communications organizer, González-Sampayo, was to show how the island(s) debt was connected to the university. With support from organizers from Comedores Sociales and other communications strategists and researchers from the ecosystem of people connected to the 2010 strike, they followed the money, conducting investigations into the relationships between specific people and the creation of the debt, which began to tell a story about who was responsible, putting names to actions made by private banks.

Banco Popular and Santander Bank were two key institutions who exploded Puerto Rico's debt. In response, students organized protests in the bank branches themselves, demanding the debt be audited. These actions helped to make popular the people's audit under the phrase "auditoria ya" (audit now). While the students brought more visibility to the need to question the archipelago's debt, the government moved swiftly against their claims. Then-governor Ricky Rosselló eliminated the commission for the audit of the debt just as the idea that some of the debt had been issued illegally was gaining traction in the public. It was clear that the administration of the island was feeling the pressure and wanted to end the dialogue.

While the 2017 strike catalyzed important shifts in how to understand and mobilize against an illegitimate national debt, many consider this seventy-three-day mobilization a failure. Students were unable to prevent budgetary cuts and only secured a year-long moratorium on them. This created a bit of breathing room though a clear path to effective action remained elusive and no further large-scale mobilizations were organized from within the UPR system. After the moratorium ended, enrollment costs doubled, and students who had participated in the mobilization were targeted and collectively punished for speaking out against the debt. Eleven students—Alexa Paola Figueroa Carrasquillo, Verónica Figueroa Huertas, Randiel Negrón Torres, Francisco Santiago Cintrón, Juan Carlos Collazo, Thaliangelly Torres González, Gabriel Díaz Rivera, Mikael Eded Rosa Rosa, Juan Carlos Silén Hernández, Ileana Marie Ayala Fontánez, and Ernesto Alejandro Beltrán Feliciano—faced criminal charges for showing up uninvited to a Board of Trustees meeting to approve the institution's fiscal plan and proposed budget cut of $241 million from 2021 to 2026.[7] Unsurprisingly, many of these students were also leaders of the mobilization, and as of 2019, the majority—seven—were still facing charges. This effort by the state to terrorize organizers for demanding a right to dialogue with the administration about the future of the institution demonstrates with infuriating clarity their exclusion by design from it.

Building Power Across Time

La Gran Huelga worked to shift certain power dynamics that limited the radical participation of movement in 2010. For example, in 2010 each encampment was responsible for organizing its own meals with varied degrees of success. But by 2017 a food committee organized three meals a day for the entire mobilization, operating out of the centrally located student center. They were able to organize more effectively in part due to the presence of members of Comedores Sociales in the committee.[8] They brought more than four years of organizing experience around sharing food in large groups of students and activist communities. The food committee had a massive pantry where they kept donated items, and several volunteers helped prepare the food and serve meals at set times each day. They were able to cater to diverse food diets and preferences, a rarity in most of Puerto Rico. Huerto Semilla (seed garden), which was established during the 2010 strike, contributed greens for salads and other items for stews occasionally to the student kitchen.

In addition to the shifts in how movement organizers were fed, female leadership had grown in 2017. Consequently, limiting gender-based violence and respecting survivors was central to the larger organizational strategy. Key to the shift was the leadership of Shariana Ferrer-Nùñez Odalys, Coralys Leon, and Verónica Figueroa Huertas, who helped to ensure that gender was front and center of all discussions within the mobilization. But as Verónica herself wrote reflecting on the strike afterward, having more female faces didn't totally change the overall culture of the movement.[9] Men still took up more space and participated in gaslighting and women had to be as aggressive as them to get heard.

Still, it is important to highlight that the 2017 organizers succeeded in decentralizing power within the mobilization. They decided that each subgrouping needed its independence from the larger body. Even the negotiating committee did not share back to the collective as it had in 2010. This was done to make it easier to organize radical actions without needing to first get the support of the whole group but, according to some, it led to less open discussions in the plenary gatherings. The decentralization in the practice affirmed fragmentation and a politic of purity.

I asked González-Sampayo what she thought could be the solution. She spoke about the need for increased vulnerability among fellow organizers and learning to organize in ways that are more sustainable by prioritizing pleasure and joy as well as the struggle. "There isn't an answer beyond the simple fact that we are the answer." González-Sampayo points to a hard truth of direct democratic practice in her reflection. Simply put, there is no fast track to the kind of freedom that includes everyone. And if we can't have fun doing it, our mobilizations won't be sustainable or effective in the long run.

I learned by witnessing the powerful mobilizations waged from within the UPR system that direct democracy slowly gathers density as it moves through a landscape. It draws participants in by the sheer magnitude of its energetic pull by the power it represents. It is a methodology for us to transform our relationship to one another, to our own agency, and to history. Whenever we want to bring diverse voices into relationship, we must go slow—slower perhaps than was desirable or even possible. We must also be willing to cultivate self-awareness, transparency, and accountability to one another, as well as be willing to make mistakes. If we are not, we wind up stuck in a loop, reproducing the systems we reject in our activism.

No matter the iteration, the student movement at the UPR was committed to building a new public sphere, one where all voices were vital. It is hard to capture the beauty revealed in the moments, however brief, where this other world was made material and mundane. Direct democracy requires a persistent commitment to listen, a challenge that grows with each passing moment and as the size of a group grows. It requires listening to repetition to develop one's capacity to hear nuance. Direct democracy can tip us toward the highest good for all when we can accept our own privileges and accept our blind spots. It requires the patience to let our individual selves evolve into collectives.

John Holloway, writing of the meaning of revolution in the neoliberal moment, suggests that key to transforming the world is how we build power. Holloway argues that the only way out of the reproduction of social relations made possible through capitalism is in refusing to "take power" as it has been understood historically. The state is not just a neutral institution but is a form of social relations that is based on the exclusion of people from power and on the separation and fragmentation of people.[10] Vital within this alternative pursuit of power is sharing power *with* others, rather than holding it over them. To make such a radical shift possible, we need to develop our own structures, our own way of doing things. Easier said than done.

Holloway didn't write about the exhausted body. I wish he had. I wrote about it at length after I participated in the 2010 mobilization, just trying to process the experience.[11] I was not on campus full-time and was not a leader. But when I was there, I never truly rested even though there was little happening for most of the day. I know my restlessness was a result of the constant threat of violent confrontation with police officers who were stationed just outside the gates around the clock and the circling helicopters that occasionally dropped propaganda onto the campus. These times were ones with a palpable sense of urgency inter-mingling with boredom and confusion. Each mobilization faced the challenge around how to prefigure or develop a community response to state led austerity while they sought to build alternatives and offer proposals to shift the tides from within challenging circumstances.

Despite the difficulties, these strikes are taken together, a movement that fuels radical imagination and radicalizes people for life. Indeed, student mobilizations have shaped organizing writ large in Puerto Rico as evidenced by the 2019 Combative Summer, which led to the oust-ing of Governor R. Rosselló. We also saw the growth of *asambleas del pueblo* (public assemblies) across the island. These spaces of open deliberation, place based, radical forms of participation made possible no doubt because of the integrity, courage, and efforts of these youth.

My hope is that these stories of organizing for an accessible, quality public education help other organizers strive for balance as they shape-shift in their understanding of power. May we all find a way to navigate the direct democracy imperatives to become ever more inclusive and decentralized as we proliferate alternatives to the logic of debt. Such change is above all about creating space for people to dream and to practice their freedom.

CHAPTER 3

Displacement and Land Privatization

Under the metaphysics of colonialism, leaving is constant. Since 2006 approximately five hundred thousand people or 14 percent of the total population have left the archipelago. In 2006, the Puerto Rican population in the United States surpassed that of the islands. In other words, we are now witnessing the largest outmigration of Boricuas in history. This recent explosion is direct result of the lack of a just recovery after Hurricane Maria.[1] But this is nothing new. Constant outmigration is a result of an unbroken line of policies designed to push out Puerto Ricans from their homeland. We have always been treated by our colonizers as unfortunate obstacles to the conquest (and later, to the progress) of the island archipelago. Frances Negrón-Muntaner termed this practice "colonial emptying."[2] Emptying the islands of Puerto Ricans has long been a desired fantasy of the Spanish and later Americans who saw the archipelago in extractive terms as a place from which to build fortunes and claim "paradise" for themselves.

I grew up in New York, long after my grandparents made the "choice" to migrate in the early 1950s. Still, I was deeply affected by these policies. I never felt at home in my suburban community. Instead, I was twice exiled—as I dramatically called it as an undergraduate. I did not grow up with my cousins in my parents' hometown of the south Bronx, nor did I have much connection to the archipelago as we rarely visited. I felt like I didn't belong; I was a "native of nowhere" as Cloé Georas so beautifully described it in her poem of the same title.[3] A Spanish term for this very diasporic conundrum is *destierro*. It literally signals the act of being torn from one's homeland. Although the term "destierro" has historically been used as a synonym for political exile, I will use it here to reflect the somatic and psychological effects of the metaphysics of colonialism.

This chapter examines the conundrum of land loss from two related but distinct cases. Drawing from my doctoral research, I offer examples of how the coastline and especially beaches, are everyday less accessible to the people of Puerto Rico. This loss is ironic since beaches are considered public space under Puerto Rico's constitution.[4] Given the recent trends toward dismantling of reserve designations, widescale abandonment of public green spaces and the rise of conservation through privatization, I think the enclosure of beaches and access to the ocean represents existential violence against a people from an archipelago. Alongside this ethnographic work, I offer a personal story of "colonial emptying" by detailing the story of gentrification in one community, Puerta de Tierra (PDT)—where my partner and I lived before, during and for a short time after, Hurricane Maria. This place is deeply significant to me because it is the same community my paternal grandmother lived in before migrating to New York City with her first two children—my father and his brother—in tow. Returning against the migratory "tides" only to be displaced from my paternal grandmother Maria's neighborhood demonstrated the difficulties in returning to one's homeland.

Beaches for the People? Limits to Coastal Access

As an archipelago located in the Caribbean, Puerto Rico's beaches are one of the biggest attractions for tourists. Consequently, Caribbean people's livelihood and dignity is often subordinate to that of the tourism economy.[5] Everyday more gated private homes and luxury apartment buildings block public access to the coastline, creating a de facto privatization of the beaches. Strategies of controlled access and intercoms rest on keeping out "unwanted" populations and operate as physical and symbolic ways to reroute movement, sustain social inequalities, and cement class and racial divisions.[6] Still, Puerto Ricans have often fought to prevent coastal privatization.

Coastlines are much more than a place to hang out and party. They are a buffer zone protecting us from storms and erosion, a nesting ground, a place of contemplation, purification, and relaxation. They are the lifeline of our island geography and our ecosystem's future depends on them. As such, they represent a key battleground against our collective destierro.

El Campamento Playas del Pueblo (Encampment beaches for the people, or campa for short) was one of the longest running mobilizations against coastal privatization; it lasted for about fourteen years (2005–19). While organizers were successful in preventing construction on these five acres of coastal property in Isla Verde, they were unable to secure its future conservation.[7] Campa was located in between the Hotel Marriott and the public bathing area or El Balneario de Carolina. The Marriott is a beachfront resort that includes a casino, restaurants, multilevel parking, and a bar. The balneario, by contrast, is a public beach accessible for three dollars per car, which also provides lifeguards, showers, gazebos, and other amenities. The five acres between these two was the site of the long-term battle.

The five acres fell into disrepair after Hurricane Hugo hit in 1989. Instead of rebuilding it, the parcel was left "abandoned" by the Carolina municipality for about fifteen years. It was slowly occupied by nature herself. Pine and almond trees grew, and the dunes returned. Then in 1996, a division of the government awarded developer, HR Properties, a long-term rental agreement for the land. The term was for fifty years with renewals up to ninety-nine years. The developer planned to build luxury condominiums as a part of the Marriott Resort as well as expand the available parking for the hotel staff and visitors.

In 2005 three activists organized a press release to denounce the construction project that was already underway.[8] They protested the fact that the developer had not conducted the required environmental impact study to demonstrate that the development was not within the *zona marítimo terreste* (ZMT; maritime land zone).[9] Not only had the Marriott failed to submit these initial feasibility studies, they had already removed a substantial amount of sand from the beach and felled trees. At the press release, the activists questioned why this ten-year-old deal was only now being made public. They denounced government officials using their powers to sell public lands through loopholes like long-term leases and alleged that they had turned it over to private hands illegally.[10]

La Compañía de Fomento de Recreativo (CFR) was the managing division of the government that signed the contract with the developer. Shortly before it was dissolved by the government, CFR began aggressively marketing lands either through sale or long-term rentals of beachfront lands to be developed. As luck would have it, the Carolina public beach was not listed among the original list of public bathing areas in 1961, thereby creating a loophole.[11] These lands were an easy mark.

Soon after the press release, a coalition formed to prevent the construction. La Coalición Playas Para el Pueblo (Beaches for the People Coalition) was comprised of neighbors and the environmental organization, Amigxs del M.A.R. (Movimiento Ambiental Revolucionario).[12] The activists occupied the lands on March 13, 2005, thus establishing campa. The first few months were marked by many direct confrontations with the police. But after an injunction that forced the Marriott to cease development, the encampment became a semipermanent fixture on the lands.

Within months of the campsite's founding, the court ruled in favor of the activists, declaring the rental contract null and void. Unfortunately, this ruling was overturned because of First Bank's invocation of the third party clause. As the bank who had mortgaged the land, it had a substantial proprietary interest in the case. Feigning ignorance about the controversy surrounding the deal and having been excluded from the proceedings, the decision was struck from the record and the case was returned to a lower court to be tried again.

Activists didn't fare as well in the second iteration of the legal proceedings for two major reasons. First, they lost the backing of the municipality when the mayor of Carolina, José E. Aponte died, and his son took office. He was much less amenable to the claims of the activists. Then the Department of Parks and Recreation (the company who took over CFR's jurisdiction) pulled out of the litigation. This left the small coalition of activists and their legal team—volunteers from the UPR environmental law clinic—to litigate the case alone. The case was then transferred from the Carolina court to one further away in Fajardo, making it harder to mobilize neighbors for protests held outside the court.

This time the courts decided in favor of the developer and First Bank in 2011, upholding the validity of the rental contract. The case was backlogged for several years in appeals but the activists were unsuccessful in overturning the ruling. Since the courts had decided in favor of the Marriott in 2011, many expected an eviction process to commence soon after, but no action was taken for years.

In contrast to the legal case, the encampment grew incrementally over the years. Organizers' efforts to reforest the landscape transformed the parcel. The first tree they planted was a ceiba, a strategy to anchor their claim. As the national tree of Puerto Rico, ceibas are protected under law. They are also an ancestral tree of great importance; across West Africa, Central America, and the Caribbean, these trees are sacred and considered home of spirits.[13] They continued to plant endemic trees and mangroves—*matabuey* (beautiful goetzea), *cóbana negra* (*Stahlia monosperma*), *guayacan* (lignum vitae), *mangle negro* (black mangrove), *mangle botón* (button mangrove), *almácigo* (*Bursera simaruba*), neem, and more—in an experimental reforestation of the coastline. Organizers even planted kitchen herbs and fast-growing vegetables in raised beds.

On the eleventh anniversary of the occupation, a group of activists from three groups that had been supporting the mobilization renamed the parcel La Reserva Natural Bosque Costero de Carolina (Carolina Natural Forest Reserve). In one way, this was part of their strategy to advocate for the space's use in perpetuity as a coastal reserve. The new name closely represented the actual state of the lands. The natural dunes had returned and plants nowhere to be found on the coast on either side of the five acres had returned. El Campamento Playas Pal Pueblo was truly a conservation proposal in action. Given that Arrecifes Pro Ciudad had secured reserve status for the ocean reef located in front of the encampment, they hoped this renaming would facilitate the expansion of the recently won reserve status onto the land.

A group of activists within the coalition began to lobby representatives in the Carolina government to take over custody of the lands. In part, it was increasingly difficult to maintain an active group direct action and improvised living community on the lands. Many of the organizers not living in the encampment were keen to pass stewardship on. An ongoing battle between those who did not live in the space but had a long-term vested interest in the struggle to protect it added more difficulty to the mix.[14]

In July 2016 the Carolina municipality sued the developer for failure to make rent payments. In the early months of the battle, the court ceded a small parcel of the five acres to Marriott for employee parking, but they never paid for it. As a result, Carolina officials announced that they would begin a process of acquiring the rights for the land from Marriott and its developer. In a way, this was great news. After thirteen years, the municipality again assumed the right to steward the land. But Marriott was going to get paid to expropriate the land that was never theirs to begin with.

Many held on to the hope that the young forest would be preserved when the municipality took over stewardship of the land. But, after the municipality took possession of the lands, they delimited the lands with fence, rope, signage, and around-the-clock security. According to the members of the organization Arrecifes Pro Ciudad, Inc., the first thing the municipality ripped out was a sign that provided a key to the educational center they were building from within the reserve. They not only removed any signs of the mobilization (tents and other improvised living spaces, raised beds, and the like) but also cleared away most of the vegetation, leaving behind only a fraction of what was once a part of the forest.

When I spoke with Vanessa Uriarte from Amigos del M.A.R., she explained that the municipality did agree to serve as custodian of the lands, but they never got the commitment in writing. Both sides had different understandings of what stewarding the land meant. From within the mobilization, it meant protect and conserve the young forest. For the municipality it meant "extend" the public bathing area. As such, upon takeover, the municipality created an enclosure and actively erased the forest from view.

For about a week the people who lived within the encampment tried to fight the bulldozers and their impending eviction. Meanwhile, other organizers who did not live in campa but were part of the coalition actively supported the municipality's takeover and assured that this was simply a clean-up phase. The longstanding rift between members of the encampment and those organizing on behalf of the cause created a confusing picture in the public and no real public support could be galvanized.

Optically, the land looked quite different after the municipal takeover. The dunes shifted inward away from the coastline, as did any evidence of conservation efforts crafted over a fifteen year-long occupation from the landscape. Although the mobilization succeeded in preventing the privatization of the land, all the most radical pieces of their reforestation work were erased.

It took me a while to go back once everything went down. I am one of the people who did not go when a call was put out to defend the lands. I regret not going to give an offering to the lands and say goodbye. When I finally returned, I had to access the beach by walking through the Marriott lobby since the informal entryway that protestors made from the bike lane was closed off. It was either that or walk about half a mile on the beach or pay the parking fee next door at the city managed public beach. When the glass doors opened, the humid salt air hit me. I recalled with sadness the battle to keep these lands from being absorbed into the tourist industry.

At first glance I was shocked. The boundary between the lands once occupied by the protestors and the parking lot was imperceptible. The municipality installed a new lifeguard tower in front of what must have been the last third of the forest. The tall pines that once were home to an observation tower reminded me of what was once there. As I walked back to the coastline, I noticed a needle in the dunes. For all the ways that the state, the media, and, yes, even the people within the coalition complained how hard it was to care for a public space, this needle signaled the arrival of other informal uses.

After I was tuned into the beaches for the people movement, it was impossible to unsee the conundrum of coastal privatization. I learned of Paseo Caribe, a residential luxury housing and commercial complex located at the entrance of the islet of Old San Juan, directly from activists I met at campa. Tito Kayak, founder of Amigos del M.A.R. and one of the group's most public faces, staged an occupation when he climbed one of the construction cranes at the Paseo Caribe project and stayed there for one week. I quickly learned like El Campamento Playas Pal Pueblo, Paseo Caribe was a battle over the boundaries of public and private property. But there are some important differences.

Development was never halted in Paseo Caribe. As such, the protest was marked by violent encounters between activists, workers, and police. But the story itself is even more deeply mired in US occupation and subsequent control of the archipelago. There are layers to the displacement and dispossession of Boricuas from this parcel of land that begin as early as 1898.[15] What's more, archaeological artifacts suggest it was a place used by indigenous people to the region. The intentions of government, military, and private and tourist industries are all comingling in this case, as they do in many examples across the archipelago.

Paseo Caribe is only steps away from the Atlantic Ocean. Online promotions for Paseo Caribe heralded the development complex as the center of the "new" neighborhood. With more than two hundred units and over one hundred thousand square feet of shopping, it's pretty much its own neighborhood. Paseo Caribe's three towers offer different options—ranging from loft-style units to villas—which were sold between half a million and $3 million each.

The area surrounding Paseo Caribe is foundational to the history and conundrum of coastal privatization.[16] Its neighbors include the hotel Normandie and Caribe Hilton. It is bordered by El Escambrón Balneario, a public-access beach located in PDT, a community within the Old San Juan district, and the public park Sixto Escobar. Paseo Caribe faces the ocean and its closest neighbor is the historic San Gerónimo Fort, which is a part of the US registry of historic places.

The Normandie opened in 1942 and was one of the first luxury hotels on the island. It closed in the 1960s, opened again briefly but it was abandoned because of the sheer cost of renovations. In 2023 the Normandie was again sold to a new developer, Normandie OZ, LLC, who struck an agreement with Miguel Romero, the current mayor of San Juan, to rent part of Sixto Escobar for thirty years. In exchange, the developer has promised to spend $20 million of its $100 million budget toward rebuilding the sports arena and building an underground parking lot to be located under the soccer field and athletic track. Although the planned underground parking lot is literally on the coast, they claim construction will not impact the shoreline. Activists fear this deal signals an impending privatization, as in the case of El Campamento Playas Pal Pueblo in Isla Verde, Carolina, which was also a long-term lease agreement.

Paseo Caribe's other neighbor is Caribe Hilton, another luxury tourist resort on the island built in 1949. Caribe Hilton was built with significant local government support and its beach was the first to be privatized in the archipelago's history. San Gerónimo Fort, located between Paseo Caribe and the Hilton—is still technically owned by the Puerto Rico government, but has long been under the care of Caribe Hilton. Instead of maintaining public access to the fort as its custodians, the hotel has padlocked the fort for decades and controlled access to it. They usually only open it for private parties and hotel functions.

Organizers established an encampment and museum documenting the history of the public lands at the entrance to the islet of Old San Juan. Their protest of the development hinged on three major issues: (1) the proximity of the development to the maritime land zone (ZMT); (2) the presence of possible artefacts of archeological value at the San Gerónimo Fort; and (3) a lack of environmental impact statements proving the safety of the development for the coast. In response to the public outcry, Secretary Roberto Sánchez Ramos of the Department of Justice announced he would investigate the claims against the proposed construction.[17]

In the hundred-page report to the governor, Sánchez Ramos found that both Paseo Caribe and Caribe Hilton were partially built on public lands. He estimated that 40 percent of the lands for the proposed development were part of the ZMT. He also found competing, coexisting claims to the land. He found fifteen different *fincas* (farms or divisions) were associated with the lands and each claimed to hold title. Thirteen public laws written by Spain, the United States, and local laws, beginning with the 1898 Treaty of Paris also made explicit claim to the lands. Finally, he also discovered that in 1920 the US government issued a long-term lease for the lands to retired US Navy Lieutenant Commander Virgil Baker and his heirs, renewable for 999 years. It cost him one dollar.

In response to the report, Governor Aníbal Acevedo Vilá suspended the developer's permits for sixty days. He ordered new surveys of the land to be conducted and appointed experts to do the work. But many did not trust that the verification strategies proposed by the governor would lead anywhere. As Mari Carmen Cruz, director of Corporacion Piñones Se Integra (COPI), a nonprofit based in Piñones—a coastal town that has also been subject to privatization and expropriation—put it, "Está diciendo que (el Proyecto) es illegal, que se construyó sobre dominio público, pero se lo tira a las agencias o a la legislature para que lo hagan legal" (They are saying that the project is illegal, and that it was built on public lands but they send it to the government agencies and the legislatura to make it legal.) Her comments reflect not only a realistic cynicism about the way that the legal process works but also local knowledge that the Puerto Rican legislature serves private interests as seen by its tendency to approve privatization schemes.

Worried about the value of their investments, San Gerónimo Caribe Project (SGCP) and First Bank brought a case against the local government. The banks demanded that the government verify that these lands were rightfully owned by Arturo Madero's company SGCP, the developer of the lands. As in the case of campa, the role of the banks in turning the tide against activists' claims was key.

Activists' fears were affirmed when the first-level courts upheld the developer's title despite the Department of Justice's findings. They argued that the lands were reclaimed from the sea (*ganados al mar*) legally when the United States expanded the Coast Guard Parcel in 1941. Furthermore, they claimed that the lands were transferred to the government tourist division La Compañia de Fomento Industrial to develop the Condado Bay Parcel in the 1950s. Consequently, they were privately owned.

In response, activists designed a people's court (tribunal del pueblo) to publicly evaluate Paseo Caribe's development and the ownership claims.[18] The proceedings lasted about two weeks. The court was composed of ex-judge and attorney Antonio Fernós, attorney Josefina Pantojas, environmental lawyer Pedro J. Saadé, economics professor Martha Quiñones, former executive director of the American Civil Liberties Union William Ramírez, PhD in history Dinorah La Luz, Nelly

Diaz, and geography professor Carlos Guilbe. The secretary of the DRNA (Departamento de Recursos Naturales Y Ambientales [Department of Natural and Environmental Resources]), Javier Vélez Arocho, also collaborated by measuring the lands.

The people's court corroborated the findings in the Department of Justice's report.[19] They found inconsistencies in the chain of ownership over time. They alleged that government title to the land was illegally obtained during the Pedro Rosselló administration. Although the Puerto Rican Tourism Company was listed as the owner in the island's property registry at the time it was sold to Paseo Caribe's developer, they could only find an affidavit on record. No original documents were presented to validate their ownership claim.[20]

The people's court spread public outrage. As a result, Puerto Rico's Supreme Court assumed jurisdiction over the case. The final decision, written on July 31, 2008, affirmed the legality of the construction. Both the decision and the dissenting opinion were long—sixty-six and seventy-seven pages, respectively. Ultimately, the court established a precedent that certain coastal lands can be sold as private property. Essentially, they argued that coastal modifications made over the course of the last hundred years in many communities in San Juan, including Condado, Puerta de Tierra, Ocean Park, Sabana, and Barrio Obrero, were all based on similar enclosures. Until this time, precedent held that lands in the ZMT were a common good that was not eligible for privatization. To decide that Paseo Caribe was built illegally on public lands would jeopardize the security of thousands of families. In other words, the court was unwilling to unravel the entire property structure on which an entire city had been built, no matter how nebulous the conditions under which these lands were secured. The justices reckon with the most flagrant abuse of public access by including in their decision that the pathway to San Gerónimo Fort be opened and maintained for public use.

By making the comparison between different parts of the city, the judges wanted to create a sense of equality, but by ignoring the conditions under which the title was gained in each case did the opposite. What remains is simply that the existence of the paper (title) assures us that the developers are the owners. Legal documentation justifying displacement erase the corruption and injustice at the heart of the system itself. In this way, title operates as a mechanism for legalized theft of the coast. Both El Campamento Playas Pal Pueblo and Paseo Caribe demonstrate how the courts serve as a mechanism of privatization. The banks also play an important role in this process.

Of course, beyond the specific details and mechanisms, the lack of access to the coastline and the ocean creates an existential problem. The coast is what anchors us to our reality as an archipelago, as an island people. What's more, the health of our coast is the health of our land. Instead of growing mangroves and quiet places of reflection, our beaches are sold for the interests of tourists and the most elite. Without a sense of ourselves as being of the islands, we falter in our steps—moving toward other landscapes and dreams—losing our ability to guarantee a future for Puerto Rico. Rapid development of the coastline also signals the lack of environmental sustainability. It's no surprise that living without access to the sea, surrounded by dense concentrations of pavement, buildings, and other surfaces that absorb and retain heat, causes much suffering. It contributes to the sense that Puerto Rico is not a place to live a dignified life.

Returning Home? Displacement and Gentrification

When I rematriated in 2016, I learned quickly that Puerto Rico is not an easy place to live. I spent my first year of rematriation crashing with friends, renting rooms, or doing trade while trying to hold onto hope of buying a space in or around San Juan that could be a home for me and the nascent CEPA. Despite my studies on coastal privatization, nothing prepared me for the devasting experience of looking for a place to live during an intense gentrification wave. The combination of Puerto Rico's already longstanding history as a tourist destination alongside the opening of a tax haven for the global elite, severely limited available long-term housing options.

When every plan had fallen through, my partner invited me to live with them in their apartment in PDT. PDT is a barrio located on the islet of Old San Juan. It was founded in the seventeenth century by poor Black and Brown people who worked in the city for Spanish and criollo elite.[21] When the commercial port was closed, the community experienced abandonment on multiple fronts. Since then, PDT has been an area coveted by developers because of its strategic and historic value and various attempts to displace the community have occurred over the years.[22] PDT is not only within walking distance of the tourist epicenter of Old San Juan but also the home to many government buildings and offices, another reason no doubt for its value for elite interests.

PDT was the last place my paternal grandmother, Maria Rosario Rivera, lived before moving to New York City in 1951. She was one of the many that formed part of Puerto Rico's (first) "great migration" who was voluntarily displaced from her homeland. I didn't ask her why she decided to leave before she passed in 2006. Neither did any of her eight children.

According to the family, the move was my grandfather's idea. He went first; she followed with her first two children. They were likely enticed by both US and local Puerto Rican government propaganda. They invested heavily in campaigns to encourage people to leave the islands for the "mainland" with a promise of better jobs, housing, and overall quality of life. But the "emptying" of Puerto Rico had little to do with improving the lives of Puerto Ricans. Instead, it was motivated by the United States' need to fill the labor shortages during and after World War II. The Puerto Rican insular government wanted to make it appear as if the agrarian to industrial transformations they were promoting were causing a decline in poverty. In fact, it was the destierro of people like my grandparents alongside a heavy sterilization program that created the ephemeral appearance of "progress."

Living in PDT was an anchor for me in difficult times, helping me to establish a sense of place. I felt connected to my *abuelita* as I imagined us crossing paths in time on the street where I lived: La Calle San Agustin, the center of PDT. I asked her why she left and heard the reply: Family. She had a difficult childhood and found hope in my grandfather. She wanted to build a life with him.

When I looked at an apartment in Falansterio, a woman whose family lived in the same housing project San Antonio where my grandmother had lived said she recognized me. Coincidence perhaps. But as much as I wanted to stay in PDT, I couldn't find a reasonably priced apartment and did not have the capital to buy and rehab one of the many abandoned buildings. So I left. But my partner continued to live in PDT, and I continued to visit and get to know neighbors.

Then, one day in 2019, a letter appeared in each of the twenty-one mailboxes, stuffed in with little care as you could expect when a business drops thousands of announcements. It came from Alejandro Mendez, the brother who served as landlord of the building, notifying the tenants of a change of ownership.[23] The letter promised that everything would remain the same except that tenants would now make rental payments to the new owner, Massri PR 2.

Within the week, my partner received another letter from the new owner Mayer Hazan notifying tenants of their eviction. He had plans to remodel the building and would need to have it vacant to complete the vision. He waived the rent payments so long as each tenant vacated the property on or before November 15, or within two months of receiving the letter. When they were finally evicted, Hazan hand delivered the security deposit to the tenants. A group of residents confronted him. I listened as he calmly told us he was just a small businessman trying to support the revitalization of the city. Hazan denied receiving any tax incentives or support from the government. He told us that New York–based Boricua artists who run the Puerto Rican Project invited him to visit the island and got him interested in investing locally. This is another example of how many of our own kin are complicit in the sale of the archipelago.

I could find little information about Hazan on the internet, but his name did lead me to a LinkedIn page where he listed himself as CEO of VMS Capital Group, a business specializing in the "acquisition of distressed residential real estate properties."[24] As it turns out, before his arrival to Puerto Rico, he made a career out of gentrifying communities in New York City. Later research publicized by Senator Maria Lourdes's office revealed he is not only an Act 22 beneficiary but also the biggest investor in the area. The last time I checked, Hazan already owned twelve properties in PDT alone. They are all under different LLCs.[25]

When Lau called a legal aid group to consult on their rights, we learned that renters had no rights in Puerto Rico. A sale always trumps a rental agreement. They were advised to give up and move on, that there was no way we could win legally against Hazan. My partner began a documentary about the situation they were facing. They even staged an action against the eviction, but eventually everyone left.

Hazan didn't work alone. He had the full support of some Puerto Ricans like the architect Mario Montijo working on the building renewal. He told a group of us who confronted him on camera that it was impossible to renew an urban area without removing the residents. While he believed it was important to preserve the historic authenticity of the area, he was solely focused on the restoration of the buildings and thought nothing about the Black and Brown poor people who have made PDT what it is. Studies have shown that whether historic designations increase or decrease gentrification depends on whether the people in the community help design the renewal process.[26]

Although both Hazan and Montijo promised that the building would be restored to its original condition, it turned out to be more lies. Months after the sale, we noticed that the building was again up for lease. Then, the remodeling began, but it was far from a restoration process. I walked into the building one day while the construction was ongoing. The entrance itself had undergone a cosmetic facelift. They added some wood detail, painted the walls, installed new light fixtures, windows, and doors. The management company of the building, San Juan 901, publicly wrote they were delayed because they discovered the building was in danger of collapse according to the evaluation performed by an engineer shortly after purchase.

In 2021 we found the apartments listed for rent as furnished residences on Zillow. The penthouse, which was rented for $500 a month in 2018, was listed for $3,300 a month. We tried to book an appointment to investigate further but no one returned our calls.

Later, we found that the whole building was listed on Airbnb managed by hospitality group San Juan 901 that describes itself as being 100 percent Puerto Rican. Their narrative erases the fact that the owner is not Puerto Rican and is an Act 22 beneficiary. San Juan 901 also tries to hide the fact that they displaced twenty-one families to launch their 100 percent Puerto Rican project. The before and after pictures of the building they proudly list on their Instagram page include the posters put up during the action staged by my partner: "Aqui Vivía Gente. Agúzate Puerta de Tierra, puede ser el próximo" (People lived here. Pay attention, Puerta de Tierra. You could be next). If San Juan 901 has its way, that's exactly what will happen.

Crashing the Dream of a Puerto Rico without Puerto Ricans

The above cases represent a small sample of the shape of displacement and gentrification in Puerto Rico today. And still, the government continues to dismantle protections of our lands. For example, in 2018, then-governor Rosselló attempted to dissolve seven natural reserves across the archipelago. These protections included more than 7,000 acres of land, 10,000 acres of marine land, and 17,300 of agricultural lands.[27] Although the Supreme Court ruled his efforts were illegal in 2021, two years have passed later, and the current Governor Pierluisi still has not reinstated the protections.

Meanwhile, housing costs have continued to rise. The COVID pandemic only worsened the trend as we witnessed an influx of privileged Americans who were now free to work and study remotely and took the opportunity to relocate. I routinely overheard conversations in English between tourists and new residents who bragged about how they "discovered" Puerto Rico because it was one of the only "borders" that was open during the pandemic.

Rather than regulate Puerto Rico's housing market and limit the proliferation of short-term rentals, the government has actively supported it. In 2018 Airbnb announced a partnership with Puerto Rico's government. As part of an effort to expand the tourist economy, they developed a new landing page and agreed to share data with Discover Puerto Rico, a destination marketing organization for the archipelago that was created through legislation in 2017. The government claimed it would boost the economy. But as my reader is probably aware, short-term rentals decrease the supply of long-term rentals making it harder for Puerto Ricans to find a suitable place to live full-time. Displacement of locals has increased at alarming rates, especially in tourist centers and historic communities.[28] For example, in 2020 in Old San Juan every single-family residence, except one, was bought by a foreign investor according to real estate agent Coral Bouret in an interview with *El Nuevo Día*. Airbnb is part of this problem. Many Airbnb listings in Puerto Rico are owned by corporations. Just ten Airbnb hosts own 611 properties across the archipelago. Just ten owners are making $18 million profit in a single year.

Each of these threads weaves a picture of land loss today in Puerto Rico. The metaphysics of colonialism is active any time that it is impossible to get to the beach even though you only live fifteen minutes away. It is seeing the violation of laws to protect our collective access to these lands; it is the disregard for the important aspect of ecosystem the transitional space of the coast represents. I see it in the eviction of yet another comrade from their home. I see it each time another landfill is established, or another shopping mall is built on top of a mountain, felling trees and erasing another small parcel of life from view.

It can be fought each time we pause to breathe in salt air and cultivate a relationship with the ocean that sustains our islands. In this way rematriation offers a way to counteract the trends of loss and emptying. While not for everyone and an immense privilege in some ways, rematriation allows us to ground ourselves in the land's wisdom through the return. Those who are here battling against the displacement and reclaiming their right to this place prevent destierro for us all. Those who are fighting the sale of everything and demanding rent controls and protections for public lands are forcing us to imagine another pathway home. There is power when we witness. There is power when we stay. When we are here, when we are present with our bodies, we can defend the land. This means hardship in some ways, but it is only when we are connected to the land that we can defend it. So many people are already crafting alternatives in response to the metaphysics of colonialism. To these paths we now turn.

* * *

Before we proceed, I invite you to take a breath with me. Give yourself a chance to feel your feet on the earth. Honor the life that flows through you. Know there is more to the story of Boriké than we have been taught. The story itself is less powerful than the way we tell it. Let us challenge our perception and look for the edges of our liberation. Know that we can shape what is to come. Consider these examples as offerings to nourish our spirits by exploring the power of the radical collective imagination. If you feel moved, I invite you to make an offering for each of the stories in your own way. Watch for shifts.

Part 2

Truth Wealth:
Pathways Toward Liberation

Comedores Sociales
Feeding Mutual Aid

Los Comedores Sociales (Community Kitchens Project of Puerto Rico) began as one arm of a larger community-based organization called the Center for Political, Economic and Cultural Development (CDPEC). As the name suggests, CDPEC sought a holistic, long-term, transformation of society through a diverse set of methods for organizing that included popular education, mutual aid, food production, travel, and participatory research. But the practice of "feeding people" through the mobile community kitchens quickly became the focal point of their vision.

This microhistory was nourished by the insights of three core members of the collective: Giovanni Roberto Cáez, Paola Aponte, and Marisel Robles. I conducted one interview with the group in Spanish at the first center of operations for CDPEC. I organized three subsequent individual conversations with Giovanni and Paola. It was a two-bedroom house located in Barriada Morales in Caguas that the group rented in late 2015. We met in the alley between the building and the other homes with the storage room of food donations behind us.

The idea for a mobile community kitchen emerged from conversations ten years earlier when a group of students that were members of the International Socialist Organization (OSI) nearing graduation at the University of Puerto Rico began discussing the future of their activism. Having organized a series of key strikes at the University of Puerto Rico, they wondered how to continue organizing once they graduated. As Marisel described it, "Queriamos ir mas alla del movimentismo y dejar de hablar de política para hacer politica" (We wanted to go beyond the movement tendency and stop talking about politics in order to make politics). In other words, they would need to work with a more diverse group of people and not only appeal to those within the movement if

69

they were to develop a long-term strategy that could change material conditions and not stay in the theoretical realm.

The group agreed that reading Hal Draper's polemical text "Towards a New Beginning: On Another Road" was transformative.[1] Draper's work provided an analysis of the failings of the Russian Revolution. He argued that socialism was little more than political doctrine being dictated from above. The Russian Revolution did not leave space for the workers themselves to decide their fate. In distinction from that earlier revolution, Draper proposed a membership-based organization based on a well-defined program.

They resonated with the "new beginning" that Draper envisioned. It was a path that was bottom-up: led by workers and militant cadres organized around a self-sustaining political nucleus. The question of how to sustain their political work in ways that would not make it secondary to their day-to-day realities was something very important to these organizers. They resonated with the idea of having their own sustenance, on not depending on someone else to fund the revolution. The students then knew that building a bottom-up movement was the task ahead of them.

Comedores Sociales began years later when Giovanni left his job as a teacher and began offering a pay-as-you-can lunch service in 2013. Core members explained that this represented a new model for producing and consuming food. The food isn't free, but there is no set fee associated with it either. There was a suggested donation, but no one was turned away if they couldn't pay for a plate. Instead, they encouraged in-kind donations to be given later to keep the exchange in circulation.

At first the project was sustained almost entirely by Giovanni. His days began around 4 a.m., and he'd spend the predawn hours cooking. He then drove the food from Cayey to Río Piedras where he served the food at the university campus and then cleaned up with the support of a few friends. Even when the administration tried to keep him from coming back because he did not have a permit authorizing him to sell food on campus, he found ways to subvert the system.

Support for the concept was undeniable. The lines were long, and the food almost always ran out in a few hours. Need among students to access reasonably priced food was high. As Giovanni explained in our conversation, "Este proyecto nació y vive de la crisis. Esto representa una oportunidad para transformar la perspectiva del poder . . . alimenta el hambre que existe y no es solamente del estómago" (This project was born from and lives from crisis. Our activism [around food] provides us with an opportunity to transform our perspective of power . . . to feed the hunger that exists, and it's not only in our stomachs). Giovanni's words reflect the perspective at the heart of the project. If we can meet our collective needs without relying on the system, we connect to the vast nature of people power and satisfy our hunger for justice.

The model spread quickly. Within the first year, various community kitchens popped up across other campuses of the public university system as other collectives copied the model. Marisel, Giovanni, and Paola described the proliferation as encouraging. They wanted to create a model that would be replicable. Instead of seeing these groups as competitors, they understood them as allies in the battle to move away from capitalist logics and into interdependence, something many are "hungry" for.

One of the core principles of Los Comedores Sociales de Puerto Rico is *autogestión*. This word is one that feels difficult to translate effectively, but it is the spirit is of doing things ourselves rather than seeking support from an external body like the government or a nonprofit. *Autogestión* is a bottom-up venture made in collaboration with the people who will benefit from it.

Through food, the collective was able to craft a bottom-up movement they had only dreamed of as students. For Comedores Sociales, real political power can only be built by working together in a horizontal relationship, never providing charity. Their goal was always to facilitate mutual aid between people. In doing so, they are creating a more just world through making politics.

Despite the difficulties inherent in creating something from very little, one of the joys of *autogestión* is healing one's sense of capacity. For example, Giovanni felt his participation in Comedores Sociales healed him from depression. It also committed him to finding ways of doing political work that were not split off from his daily life. Contrary to popular opinion, the framework of "mutual aid" did not have its origins in anarchy. Giovanni drew inspiration from a psychiatrist based in Ocean Park who spoke about mutual aid and self-effort as conjoined practices. He explained, "La sanación es muchas cosas. Estar bien, implica que uno haga un esfuerzo" (Healing can be a lot of things. Being well implies making an effort yourself). This approach to mutual aid might be simplistically understood as self-help, but I think it speaks to a deeper understanding of how change occurs. It's not charity, which relies on one person or side being vulnerable or a victim. Each of us has work to do and our commitment to it is necessary for mutual aid to exist.

Paola similarly described Los Comedores as healing. This healing was potentiated through the relationships made in the act of donating supplies that make Los Comedores possible. She explained, "Food is a vehicle for generating experiences that cultivate empathy and build bridges between people. When people donate, it's a very powerful experience. Sometimes, we cry together." Paola is speaking here to the healing that comes from the exchange of gifting food so that many others may eat. In doing so, a part of oneself is healed. In this way, Los Comedores created the possibility for an intimate encounter among strangers.

The lunchtime gatherings created by the collective also became a way to sustain movements and inform political processes. Los Comedores created an informal bridge between different generations of student-organizers to learn from one another. Indeed, it helped to rupture the usual amnesia that occurs within student mobilizations because of the graduation cycle. For example, when students organized the 2017 strike at the University of Puerto Rico, members of Los Comedores played a supportive role. They quite literally fed the movement, providing food at plenary sessions and general meetings for the student body *before* the strike was approved. They also nurtured the movement through mentorship and active participation in the organizing process.

Los Comedores Sociales's influence is undeniable. As I described in chapter 2, the strikers created a food coordination committee that prepared three meals a day for all the distinct encampments in the student center. The combination of donations of preprepared meals and what students prepared from their stock of reserves always included a vegetarian option, and often included food that was harvested from the student garden Huerto Semilla. Los Comedores's support of the strikers and involvement in the food committee transformed the meaning of coming together to eat, encapsulated in the slogan that became popular during this strike, "Yo no como austeridad, yo cocino dignidad" (I don't eat austerity! I cook dignity). Overall, Los Comedores succeeded in providing a model for exchanging resources in crisis, nourishing the new organizers with wisdom and sustenance.

Just before Hurricane Maria hit, the group was entering into a collaboration with university-based comedores. Rather than continue to run parallel to each other, they decided to join and form a larger project. The hurricane season of 2017 had other plans and derailed their launch. It was after Hurricane Irma (the storm that preceded Hurricane Maria) that the group put together its first community kitchen, which was a foreshadowing for things to come. As Giovanni explained, "the population was totally different. [Instead of working with university students], we had to deliver food to some folks who lived in a nearby shelter and had curfew. No one talks about that, but it was an important part of what we would do later." Little did they know that the storm would enable them to scale up to another level of feeding solidarity through the first Centro de Apoyo Mutuo (Center of Mutual Aid or CAM).

When Hurricane Maria hit, they were able to respond very quickly to their community's needs after the storm. Within a week, Los Comedores in collaboration with Urbe a Pie—an urban restoration project based in Caguas—launched the first CAM. They moved from renting to occupying like many other groups at this time, signaling an understanding that, in times of crisis, rent is not just or accessible. They took over an old social security government building that had been abandoned for over thirty years in the urban center of Caguas. In its place they offered weekly ear acupuncture clinics and daily hot meals.

Like Los Comedores, the core goal of CAM was to feed the community.[2] They offered a hot meal to over two hundred people daily. The group was clear that they were not giving aid but providing a structure wherein each person might enter a relationship of mutual support. Through CAM, they were reminding community members that the real power was among us, as a people united. As Paola explained it, "People were seeing us respond before the government. Someone even proposed that we should be the decision-making body, replacing the government." She glowed with joy as she told me. And for good reason; what the group has been able to achieve is impressive.

Los Comedores also grew because of the new initiative. They had more members and more volunteers. When I went to visit Paola and interview her in Río Piedras in 2019, I marveled at the fact that she was able to stop serving food and just sit down and talk to me. During the short lunchtime service period, three volunteers took over for others who had been working earlier in the day. The model began to thrive, reflecting the principled origins and thoughtfulness that the early members had put into creating the structure.

After the pandemic swept Puerto Rico, hunger became an even bigger problem across the archipelago. Thousands of people found themselves out of work and stuck in their homes. Since Los Comedores Sociales was already organizing *compras solidarias* (solidarity groceries), they were able to track the growing problem. Suddenly, they were spending $60,000 a month on groceries. Aware that they could not meet the growing need, they organized a protest called Caravana por la Vida (Caravan for Life) to demand more COVID testing and resources to meet the new demand like providing more food stamps and expanding coverage for unemployment. They created a caravan of vehicles to circumvent the stay-at-home orders, asking that folks only ride with people from their household to not risk spreading the virus at the event. Protestors who planned to come by foot or bike were advised to come wearing masks and to socially distance.

After leaving the first stop on the caravan's route, Giovanni was arrested by officers who claimed the speaker system was a violation of the curfew order. In the videos recorded by protestors, the police were angry and looking for someone to scapegoat. After repeated questioning and harassment if he was the leader, the videos show Giovanni attempting to get into the vehicle he came in, only to be arrested by the officers. One officer can be heard saying, "Our patience has run out," as they take Giovanni away.

Giovanni was released that night, and the charges were dropped. Inside the jail he was recorded singing a phrase that became the group's campaign: "Yo lo que quiero es comida pa' los pobres" (I want food for the poor). Under the slogan "Comida pa' los pobres" the group raised over $30,000 for *compras solidarias* in the days after the arrest. In a recent documentary, Giovanni says that he developed the song to tell the officers why he was arrested. "I wanted to get into their heads. I wanted those cops to go to sleep that night hearing my song."[3]

Soon after, at CAM Caguas, Los Comedores unveiled a food cooperative called El Super Solidario (The Solidarity Supermarket). Once or twice a month on Saturdays since January 2020, they open the market, and anyone can come and buy groceries at lower than supermarket prices. In addition to canned foods, they also buy directly from farmers for local harvests and sell local eggs. In the market, signs feature the names and locations of the farmers and projects that they have sourced food from. The new cooperative is slowly branching out and making local, high-quality food available at accessible prices.

Alongside all the gorgeous projects and organizing efforts that Los Comedores Sociales was leading, they were mobilizing to stay in the building they occupied after Hurricane Maria. They spent years trying to identify the owner of the building so they could negotiate the transfer of title. Public records are not often updated, and private owners are not easy to locate. In the meantime, they continued to organize. They developed petitions to show all the support the center had. Then, Jay Fonseca, a mainstream journalist who has his own show, featured them as part of an investigative piece on disaster capitalism. He helped to expose that the building was bought two years before Hurricane Maria by the Morgan Reed Group, the same Act 22 beneficiary who bought a public school in Puerta de Tierra. The news coverage was critical of the impact of disaster capitalism. Like Morgan Reed Group, when wealthy individuals and businesses are offered tax incentives, they can leave the buildings and parcels of land they own "as is" since they face no penalty when leaving properties uncared for.

The visibility worked. The chief operating officer of Morgan Reed Group, Brian Tenenbaum, reached out to the group. He was very unhappy with the publicity. Comedores Sociales had been preparing for this moment. First they asked that the building title be transferred as a donation given the resources the group had already put into rehabilitating the building. Tenenbaum refused. The group entered a formal mediation with him, and they agreed to buy the building for $65,000. After ten years of organizing efforts, CAM is theirs, and really, this is a win for all of us in Puerto Rico. The purchase of the building is both an end and a new beginning for the group. Now, without the fear of facing eviction, their efforts can only grow to ensure mutual flourishing and full bellies for all.

Los Comedores Sociales is a group that continues to demonstrate how to feed solidarity through organizing that is grounded in a commitment to care for others. Their leadership is awe-inspiring. The constant growth of the group is evidence that they are feeding a world beyond the colony by building and satisfying the hunger for collective power.

Patio Taller

Crafting Afro-Diasporic Possibilities

Patio Taller (Workshop Yard) is a community arts space located on a family *parcela* in San Antón, Carolina.[1] There's no signage announcing its location. You must be intimately connected to distinguish its entrance just off an industrial road lined with tire shops and mechanics' garages. Home to mapenzi chibale nonó and mulowayi iyaye nonó's family for three generations, Patio Taller is grounded in this legacy. Patio Taller is a place of creative sustenance for the sisters who are performance artists known as Las Nietas de Nonó. From this physical space, they craft black feminist, ecological historic futures by nurturing intergenerational community with their neighbors, family, and close allies in the present.[2] Although the art that mapenzi and mulowayi create is not the focus of this piece, it is impossible to separate it from the work they do on their family parcela. This microhistory is based on a series of conversations I had with the sisters over a period of about a year.[3]

The remaking of a family inheritance into an arts space was born from a simple necessity: mapenzi was looking for somewhere to live. The family parcela was vacant so she decided to return home. Both mapenzi and mulowayi had spent significant time there as children. They were raised between the Manuel A. Pérez housing project in Río Piedras and the parcela located in the San Antón neighborhood of Carolina.

To prepare for moving in, they first had to clean out the home because their aunt—the last resident—had left a lot of things behind. Faced with the pain of the rapid transformations of capital and the accumulation of waste, she turned her home into an informal recycling center. mapenzi explained that her aunt couldn't make sense of the idea that we just throw things out when we no longer "need" them. She believed that there was a use for everything.

The effect was palpable. mulowayi said she noticed her aunt aging rapidly under the weight of this shift and believed her struggles were a result of the pain she experienced as people became increasingly disconnected from the earth. Honoring the legacy of their aunt is crucial to both mapenzi and mulowayi. A concrete way that translates to their work is reusing found materials. They work very intentionally with what they have at their disposal when creating. Health is at the baseline of their creative collaboration. For black people living on the margins of capital, abandonment is a common experience. For mulowayi, the work of making from what has been left behind is a way of honoring the commitments of their relations.

In the archives left by their aunt, the sisters encountered pieces of their own family history for the first time. They found fragments that had been actively silenced by many of their elders, an issue that mulowayi described as "the pain it took to remember." Through the archives and the parcela itself, they reconnected with memories broken by poverty, racism, and spiritual oppression. They saw a real possibility there in the old archives to transform *too much pain* into art and insight. By working with stories that were not passed down to them directly, they began to alchemize the past and redefine their future. All the while, their presence began to transform the land they were raised on.

Their work on the land is not a unidirectional movement. The land also demands certain work from them as mapenzi explained to me. mulowayi described it as a process of uncovering and reconnecting fragments through observation. mulowayi explained, "El espacio mismo requiere que se trabaja a nivel espiritual . . . Es un proceso de destapar. De hacer fijo de la memoria fragmentada. Se descubre cosas mientras se mira" (The space itself requires that we work on a spiritual level. Our memories are fragmented but we discover things simply by looking). This practice of observation is simple on one level, but also quite spiritually significant. When one can open to the wisdom surrounding them, mysterious resonances between self and other and now and here, then and there can emerge.

mapenzi continues, "When I listen to them, I hear that being in reciprocity with the land also gives life, providing creative direction and purpose." It suggests that one can remember by deeply listening and then moving in rhythm with the wisdom that reveals itself. By accepting that guidance and acting on it, one can experience a deeper relationship with the land. For example, to adequately care for fruit trees, one must make juice so the abundant harvest will not be wasted. In turn the tree flourishes, and our collective interdependence strengthens.

The sisters repeatedly underscored that the practices they carry out are not new. Rather, they are neighborhood traditions essential for their survival as black people living on the margins—geographically and economically—of empire. For example, the parcela was home to their paternal grandfather who worked as a farmer on the land and their grandmother—a *curandera* (traditional healer who often works with herbs to cure spiritual imbalance), mother and midwife who was well respected by the community. This pair left an indelible impression on the parcela itself. They feel it is their job to carry out these legacies.

mapenzi emphasized their work was not about following trends: "My grandparents were sustainable, they were agroecological. They didn't call it that, but they already had practices that are now popular." They cared for animals, grew plants without pesticides, and lived in relationship with one another. They made juices out of the fruits, preserves, and canned foods. As a result, they incorporate food, community, and plant-based infusions into their performances and the activities hosted in Patio Taller. In this way, their artistic practice is healing for the family—both blood relations and others who share their identity as black people—as a whole.

Indeed, honoring one another and living together in a way that amplifies our collective wealth is a daily practice for the sisters. mulowayi talks openly about not having a roadmap, or formal plan, and saw it as important for their philosophy: "We want to distance ourselves from the institutional way of doing things and not become attached to a rigid structure." Although they have begun planning in later years, the listening and acting at the heart of their early practice remains central.

For example, the first activity they organized in Patio Taller was a theater workshop. The idea came from a casual conversation they had between some of the youth in the community and themselves as they moved mapenzi into the space. When they discovered a shared love for theater, the sisters decided to offer a weeklong full-day workshop for over thirty children held within just a few weeks of the conversation. Since then, the children of the barrio have grown fond of the space.

mapenzi laughed as she explained that it has become the plaza of the barrio where the children feel safe to come and go as they please. The sisters likened the philosophy of emergence to the Caribbean practice of improvisation. As a region where systems are known to simply not work, improvisation is a vital skill necessary to survive in the Caribbean.

As mapenzi explained, "Patio Taller is in constant change, as we are. When we travel, the use changes, the people change. Patio Taller is a space for cultivating horizontal relationships and learning together." The sisters have applied this improvisational attitude to their own relationship with the parcela, as well as any collaboration that takes place there. Moving away from charity models of "assistance," they fostered instead mutual aid that relies on the notion that each person has something to share that is of value. Listening for the intersection between all peoples' needs and abilities was the basis for their collaborations.

They underscored again that mutual aid isn't a new practice but rather a continuation of a legacy. Even the structures on their family parcela were built in community. In this way, mulowayi described the parcela as "a space that gives us everything." The shift required was to begin from the baseline that abundance exists everywhere. And over the years, they have reversed the notion of "scaling" that is at the heart of most people's vision of "growth." Rather than taking on more, they work deeply at a small scale, growing horizontally. Most of their events are held in the community and for the community and the event is shared by word of mouth, not on Facebook or Instagram.

This concentration of energy and decision to collaborate with the San Antón residents is intentional. As mapenzi explained, "We want to work with our neighbors because we know that these are the relationships that will last. If you plan an event and a person comes in from a far-away town, then well it may be a success in the short-term, but then they leave and never come back." Neighbors share in the daily life with one another, and each event grows transformative power, intimacy, and support. That's why the sisters describe their work as being "entre nosotras" (among us).

In a world where poor and black communities are often the subject of intervention, the choice to move toward autonomy, to move inward instead of outward, is radical indeed. Their idea of "us" goes much further than their blood relations. Instead of affirming the individualist idea of a "home" as belonging to one's family, they have instead shared it openly with their neighbors and loved ones. As a result, Patio Taller has been the site of innumerable creative explorations. They have organized artistic retreats, as well as workshops on mending old clothes and how to kill and eat iguanas (an invasive species in Puerto Rico). They have filmed music videos and more.

mulowayi didn't like the idea of aspiration that I brought up when I asked them about their vision of social change. She shook her head,

"A vision is too far away. What we have closest to us is what powers change." She spoke of listening to the space and one's body to figure out what can be sustained. This helps them always maintain an attitude of growth in efforts to improve their existence: "We see what our bodies can sustain, and then remake the process."

There's a good deal of magic in this act of looking and feeling beyond the facade of things and defining one's path in terms of mystery. We spent a lot of time talking about mystery in my first interview with the siblings. I asked for a definition and mulowayi offered this powerful definition.

> El misterio es todo aquello que surge de un lugar no planificado donde se manifeste algo vital. De lo que no tenemos razón para explicarlo. Tu intuición te diriga. Le coge vida. Siguendo tu intuición sin cuestionarlo tanto.

> (Mystery is anything that comes from an unplanned place where something vital manifests. Where we don't have reason to explain what transpired. Mystery is where one's intuition directs and takes on its own life. It's following that instinct without questioning it.)

Las Nietas de Nonó let their artistic explorations be guided by mystery. In my experience, mystery requires a receptivity and ability to listen to a deeper wisdom. Each person has access to this wisdom, what mulowayi calls intuition if we are listening to the knowledge beyond words and are not trapped by our mind's desire to know. When we can follow the feelings and hunches without doubt, we can access the mystery needed to create a world beyond this one.

mulowayi and mapenzi also provide examples of how mystery has shaped their artistic practice. One powerful example came from the first performance they created about their family in 2014, *Manual del bestiario doméstico* (Manual of the domestic bestiary). It is a story based on their movements between the Manuel A. Perez housing project, school, and prison in Guayama, to visit the incarcerated men in their family. It speaks to several experiences that are central to the systemic racism experienced in black communities within Puerto Rico, including discrimination, mass incarceration, drug trafficking, violence, and poverty. As they were performing the piece in Patio Taller, a cousin from prison called during a monologue given by a prisoner. "We looked at each other, asked the audience and decided to answer." From the very first performance, mulowayi says, "[Our art] has opened a path. All the keywords of our work were there: sickness, being/existence, spirituality, mind, school, prison, body, crisis." Other mysterious examples speak of impossible coincidences—two people writing the same thing at different historical moments, only to be discovered later in the family archives.

Another mysterious moment occurred when a relative spoke about experiencing a history that they did not live through, what some scholars call "postmemory" whereby past traumas are carried by survivors' family members.[4] In terms of new research in epigenetics, these traumas live in the body, carried in the expression of one's genes. They are not permanent changes but take awareness and practice to transform. By tracking the resonances and repetitions of postmemories in their own lineage, they rupture the link and create something new. Whether you believe in magic or not, a real mysterious alignment is anchored by mapenzi and mulowayi's careful attention and intention. Their belief that from the very first step everything we need is already present and that we know on some deep, cellular level where we are going is a very powerful approach.

In 2020 the sisters invited neighbors, friends, and community members to participate in a renaming ceremony they held for themselves on the parcela. From their own perspective, this was a culmination point in their own healing. In their artistic practice they always used Nonó (their grandfather's nickname) in an instinct to leave behind the slaveholder names they were born with. But this naming ceremony fully released any hold these names had on them, and they took on their current names mapenzi and mulowayi. Recognizing and honoring the sacrifices their family had made and all they had survived as enslaved peoples, they returned the names they were given and assumed their new identities. At the ceremony, the sisters explained the meanings of their names and why they had taken them and agreed to uphold and assume responsibility for living out the essence of their new identity. These names reflected their own research into their ancestral origins and their own efforts to translate their essential identity as they had come to know themselves into African names.

I can say that it was truly an honor to witness them claim their freedom. It was a moment of possibility and hopefulness that we can transform without losing who we are and where we have come from. This naming ceremony held on the land that has served as the familial home for generations is a dream that many of those in the African diaspora can't imagine. I feel in every fiber of my bones that time was pierced in that moment, and the ancestral future was anchored. I believe our sense of possibility grew collectively just by witnessing this bold act of self-determination.

Post-Maria Note

When I asked mulowayi and mapenzi how their project shifted after the hurricane, they shrugged. For them, there were mainly continuities between pre- and post-Maria in Puerto Rico. Any changes were merely in intensity and scale. For example, after the storm, no organization or government official came to San Antón to help. In the sisters' experience, that kind of abandonment was nothing new. If anything, it motivated them even more to work at "home" in more collective and expansive ways. Just before the storm, the sisters, along with other members of the community, submitted a proposal to the local government to develop a new community center La Conde in the community school Carlos Conde Marín, which was closed at the end of the 2016–17 school year. Most people in San Antón and in the neighboring barrios (La Araña, Betania, Santo Domingo, and San Just) remembered attending this primary school for at least two generations. Some sent their own children there and most remembered walking to it before the communities surrounding it were physically divided by the construction of a highway in the 1990s.

The early idea was to gain governmental approval to craft an ecological school that better reflected the interests of the community members. They imagined a learning environment in harmonious relationship with the earth, with a focus on how to be in healthy relationships with the land and water. After Hurricane Maria hit, the proposal was stalled on the government level.

Rather than wait for approval, they began the rehabilitation of La Conde themselves. They held brigades in 2018 and, with the support of La Maraña—a nonprofit that supports citizen participation in rehabilitation processes—facilitated a community design process. As a result, the community decided to start to plant a fruit tree forest in the land surrounding the buildings and structures of the school. The group born from this process is known as Las Parceleras Afrocaribeñas. They describe themselves as a barrio movement of black women who lead social justice, climate, and cultural justice work from San Antón.

The group was formally incorporated in 2019 and all were a part of La Conde. The school is at the heart of the barrio's transformation. They imagined a citizenship participation project grounded in antiracist and ecological principles.

Las Pareceleras Afrocaribeñas first began to rehabilitate the "home economics" classroom. mapenzi explained that it was important to reimagine this aspect of life first to birth a new world. Historically, household management has been forced on girls as part of their social-ization within patriarchy, leading in larger part to the domestication of their dreams. But the kitchen table can also be a radical place as black feminists have taught us.[5] It is the center, the place where women have historically gathered, nourished, and planned their liberation.

In line with the black feminist kitchen table practices that are at the heart of the rehabilitation of the old home economics classroom, the group planted fruit trees around the building and in the commu-nity. The fruit tree forest was integral to this work. It not only provided green space (and eventually, food) but also offered a space to connect to the earth, to learn from and be taken care of in return. The decision to begin in this way joined together the future and the past, for many generations the people in and around La Conde have tended the land, only recently moving away from these traditions.

Over the last three years La Conde has grown steadily as community members have been working on the building and collectively design-ing the project. Through Las Parceleras Afrocaribeñas, they continue the neighborhood efforts to secure the legal rights to the building. In December 2020, Las Parceleras Afrocaribeñas was granted legal cus-tody of the Carlos Conde Marín school. They are now in the first phase of renovating the space as a multipurpose community hub.

As a result of their collaborations with La Conde, Las Nietas de Nonó have noticed that they are shifting toward intergenerational work. In their last ceramic workshop, the youngest participant was seven years old while the oldest was fifty years old! mapenzi said it was so important for children to see adults learning things, because it helps to demy-stify the notion that adults know everything. Being witnessed in this way also creates more humility for adults, something they both felt was needed to build stronger relationships across generations. Whether in Patio Taller, crafting their own artistic projects or participating in com-munity led initiatives, mapenzi and mulowayi are committed to black liberation. They live with courage, creativity, and power, inspiring oth-ers to do the same.

La Colmena Cimarrona
Farming for Freedom

"We wanted to grow food where they said we couldn't." This short matter-of-fact statement by Ana Elisa Perez-Quintero summarizes the seed intention of La Colmena Cimarrona (Maroon Beehive), a food sovereignty and black abolitionist project based in Vieques. Although there is a vibrant and growing agroecology movement on the main island, many outright shunned Vieques as a possible site for farming, alleging that healthy food couldn't be grown in such contaminated soil. In a place where the lands and waters were poisoned by long-term US Navy use of the island as a site for war games, Ana's comment speaks to the urgency of cultivating futures that offer healing, sustenance, and inspiration for local Viequenses.[1] Refusing such purity, La Colmena Cimarrona has cultivated incredible harvests and organized community around food and racial liberation. This microhistory was nurtured by intermittent conversations I had with Ana Elisa Perez-Quintero and Jorge Cora over a three-year period.[2]

During a workshop the duo gave with Universidad Sin Fronteras (University without Borders), Ana Elisa explained that they started to call their work *agricultura cimarrona* (maroon agriculture) to distinguish themselves from a new back-to-the land movement that calls itself *neojíbaro*.[3] Although it's the case that young farmers who identify as *neojíbaro* are doing so to reclaim the legacy of self-sufficiency they associate with these ancestors, Ana and Jorge critique this naming. Ana told participants, "That legacy ignores the wealth of knowledge and value that our African ancestors held. It also ignores the fact that racism informs who has access to lands to till, to work in agriculture." In other words, to center a back-to-the-land movement on *el jíbaro* ignores the vast racial privilege of those who are able to reclaim lands under the flag *"neojibaro."* It also ignores the overwhelming class privilege of this movement as most of the people within it are rehabilitating lands owned by their families.

Land ownership is a notoriously opaque topic in Puerto Rico. Racial demographics of land ownership in Puerto Rico are not easy to track, not only because of the politics of whitening and racial passing in the archipelago but also because the census and other statistics do not record this data. The census's focus is on the size of farm, yields, and age of farmers, as well as the amount of time they have been farming.[4] It is generally accepted that Puerto Rico is always behind the United States, largely because of the colonial relationship that has funneled money and resources out of the island for more than a century. In studies performed on title ownership in the United States, 98 percent of all lands are owned by whites.[5] One can imagine a similar picture for the archipelago.

As Ana Elisa explained, "Por eso agricultura cimarrona, por que es mucho más que un asunto de raza, es también el poder escapar, el poder construir un mundo nuevo en un palenque" (That [focus on social inequality] is why we call it 'maroon agriculture,' because it's much more than a racial issue. It's also the power to escape, the power to construct a new world in a living community). For the duo, growing food is part of this pathway to freedom. It allows one to "escape" from the current conditions of dependency and make something new.

The African legacy in Puerto Rican agriculture is extensive but rarely acknowledged. La Colmena Cimarrona reclaims foods that come from our African ancestors and are more resistant to climate change. This work is also necessary because of the extreme weather conditions and long periods of drought that people in Vieques are facing today. For Ana Elisa, this work is about continuing the legacy of marronage that persisted in the face of forcible enslavement and displacement. She told me of the story of people who transported their ancestral foods as seeds hidden in braided hair of mothers and children. The seed of these plants represented that little hope that was left to have something familiar, something from home, that could ground them in an unfamiliar context. As Ana Elisa described, "Most people don't know that many people were enslaved precisely because they had agricultural knowledge, which colonizers found very valuable." For Ana and Cora, this recovery is central.

I visited Finca Conciencia a short time after Ana Elisa moved to Vieques. The project was started by Cora in 2008 when he came to Vieques from his hometown Arroyo on the south coast of the main island to buy queen bees from Mike Diaz. Cora had already been a beekeeper for years. When he arrived, he was offered a job and decided to stay. As a part of the deal, he convinced Diaz to let him use approximately three acres of a nine-acre property in Monte Carmelo for beekeeping and farming. Cora smiled as he told the story, "Creo que el pensé que no iba a poder con tanta tierra difícil" (He didn't think I would be able to handle so much difficult land). But in about five years he turned it into a productive farm.

Ana Elisa partnered with Cora in 2014 after taking a workshop with him in Vieques. Although new to the island, she was an experienced organizer. She helped to develop an educational project and incubator for environmental campaigns known as GAIA and built three urban gardens that served as a hands-on laboratory for students. During the strike at the UPR in 2010 when I met her, she was one of the people who brought visibility to the issue of food sovereignty during the mobilization and was one of the cofounders of the first garden planted on the campus as part of the strike.

With Ana's vision and organizational skills, the farm grew exponentially. Together, Ana and Cora intensified the "promoter" training offerings in agroecological farming methods and beekeeping to interested neighbors and allies who trekked to the site. They were also able to expand the vegetable production of the farm and sold to local restaurants and folks living in Vieques.

Although a small operation, the impact of this work cannot be overstated. Puerto Rico's high level of food insecurity is well known. Vieques's situation is further exacerbated by a highly unreliable ferry service to deliver goods from the main island, over 80 percent of which had already been imported from the United States. Indeed, the entire island of Vieques is considered a food desert. Add to this the winds, low rainfall, and periods of drought, and the situation is very challenging to say the least.

Visiting Finca Conciencia is akin to entering an alternate field of possibility. It is located on a mountaintop called Monte Carmelo with a near perfect 360-degree view of ocean and coastline below. Monte Carmelo is a site of resistance to imperialism and is known locally as *monte de abejas* (bee mountain) since it was where bees were deployed against US Navy in the long battle to get them off the island.

Cora recounted many stories of strangers showing up to ask about purchasing the property. Sometimes they would even enter the property unannounced. He explained, "Los gringos siempre querían esta propiedad por la vista" (North Americans wanted this property for the view). Still, Finca Conciencia is a stronghold for another world.

Ana and Jorge lived in radical simplicity on the property. They did not depend on services from the state. The house-workshop had few ceilings save for two small rooms that were closed off. The kitchen, both with traditional *fogón* (hearth) and gas stove, invokes distinct eras and ways of engaging place. The neighbors lend them an extension so they can power a few appliances with electricity, but they mainly live without it. They collect rainwater and eat what they plant, supplemented by the occasional fish they buy from local fishermen and dried products bought in bulk.

Jorge calls himself a maroon, even though the formal system of enslavement ended before he was born. He identifies with the fugitive lifestyle and proudly admits he dropped out of school, preferring to work the land from an early age. He prefers being slightly off the map, quietly working on the farm.

Both Ana and Cora saw their work as abolitionist. Cora said, "Yes, we are abolitionists because we want to abolish prisons. They serve only to keep us segregated, but we also must abolish racism, abolish our energy systems, our housing, and even our understanding of health." In other words, for the duo, it was essential to transform these systems completely and from below like the maroons.

Their focus on blackness has led them to be interested in broader cross-Caribbean exchanges in a region where Puerto Rico tries to be exceptional racially. In contrast, La Colmena's work is trans-Caribbean. The duo makes regular visits to the Dominican Republic and Haiti to share tools and knowledge with their island kin. When I interviewed them, they recently visited Culebra and were marveling at how similar the experiences were for those on the smaller islands of the Puerto Rican archipelago.

Despite the long-term vision of their work, Ana and Jorge don't hold title to the land they work. Cora, who has been on the land for more than ten years, was gifted it in a verbal agreement. Once the "owner" died, the children tried to come and take the land from him. They brought him to court. I was shocked and asked, "You went to court? What were you going to do?" He responded, "They don't have papers either, so I figure it's just as much mine as theirs. On the day of the hearing, the other side didn't show up."

Like Cora, many people lack title although they have lived on lands for generations. This is especially complex in Vieques because of the long-term presence of the military. The issue of property ownership became a subject of public debate after Hurricane Maria when about 40 percent of people who applied to FEMA for aid to repair their homes after storm damage were denied because they could not produce the paperwork that the US government requires to validate claims.[6] Many times, families live on land for generations without holding title.[7]

Residents like Cora's predecessor likely came and cleared the land and began working it, effectively laying claim to it.[8] At the same time, adverse possession laws in Puerto Rico are extremely retrograde making it difficult to assert ownership claims if an absentee owner shows up wanting to displace the family who has been living on it for generations. The generations the family has been there, the work that one has put into it, all are other ways of accounting what belongs to whom. We must also remember that property is after all a colonial invention, a sleight of hand to steal land that our indigenous ancestors knew belonged to itself. We are merely stewards working toward a reciprocal relationship, deeply understanding, and honoring the life the land makes possible in us.

Post-Maria Note

Finca Conciencia suffered extreme damages after the storm. The rainwater catchment system was destroyed and since the workshop did not have many walls, appliances and many of their possessions flew in the high winds. Ana described it as a very overwhelming moment. But within a few months, they began rebuilding with the support of various groups and allies like Black Dirt Farm Collective, Climate Justice Alliance, and Boricuá. Boricuá is a nonprofit ecological agricultural group bringing together farmers across the archipelago of Puerto Rico who are committed to a vision of farming that exists in harmony with nature. They organized many brigades after the storm to assist members of their network across the archipelago to get back on their feet. While the farm was in this redevelopment process, La Colmena expanded quickly to attend to the needs of the people in Vieques.

A group of five women founded El Panal, establishing a community kitchen and donation center in the town of La Esperanza. Taking over a part of a church's buildings, they created a space dedicated to their own healing and building community. All the women were educators. None fit the typical profile of an organizer against the US Navy. They described themselves as the women who stayed at home, cared for the children, and cooked during the more than thirty-year mobilization. They offered ear acupuncture, hot meals, and various workshops to support the community. Although affiliated with the wider network of CAMs on the main island, they saw their work as independent.

When I came to visit a few months after the hurricane to offer a workshop on tinctures, El Panal had been running weekly community health clinics for more than a month. At each gathering a meal was provided alongside a hands-on workshop related to health coordinated for the benefit of the community. They were building a garden in the land behind the church and had a very large supply of canned foods and water in the kitchen that they had received as donations. Almost every week, a visitor came and led a workshop of some kind.

More than four thousand Viequenses had left the island in 2018 after the hurricane, and four years later, that trend continues with approximately only nine thousand people remaining on the island. While the numbers of Viequenses decline, the population of North American folks has grown. The surge in wealthy, absentee owners, however, means that prices for land have skyrocketed and buying land for farming has become all but impossible.

Together, the women who began El Panal are writing a book about Hurricane Maria and offering activities to youth. Ana Elisa spent much time traveling because of opportunities that emerged after the storm. This allowed her to meet others organizing around themes of land access, food, agroecology, and cooperatives with the women from different regions: from Chiapas' Zapatista communities to Cooperative Jackson in Mississippi.

After her return, Ana decided to leave her role as cocoordinator of Finca Conciencia and start a new project. Ana is now working full-time to develop twenty-five acres of abandoned agricultural lands that she is renting from the Puerto Rican government. The focus is to develop programs for youth without access to lands to learn agroecology. The idea is to continue building alternatives, but to make sure they are connected in some way to ensure their longevity.

On the newly acquired lands, La Colmena Cimarrona is germinating a learning space. One of the members of El Panal, Elda, gifted its name El Centro Agroecológico Popular La Semillera (Popular Center of Agroecology, The SeedBed). Within less than two years, they have installed a rainwater and solar-panel system to attend to Vieques's very dry and hot climate, showers, and an area for washing harvests. The shower area is for brigades, events, and camping, as well as for the workers themselves. In addition, they have been planting trees to support planned crops with shade and water retention. This is a key part of making the farm a place where many people can learn together and pollinate liberation with visitors and Viequenses alike. They have already planted lemon trees, *icacos* (paradise plum), and other drought-resistant, heat-loving plants, including *anones* (sugar apple), *acerola* (Caribbean cherry), and *guanábanas* (soursop). A key battle for them has been the droughts, but they continue with a force and determination that is incredible.

This is a mere sampling of the freedoms being born through La Colmena Cimarrona. Together, grounded in their connection to the earth, La Colmena works for food, connection, antiracist futures, and sovereignty. Their work reminds me of all the sweetness inherent in abolition work. From seed to root to blossom, there is immense beauty and satisfaction for those making a path to freedom.

El Hormiguero

An Okupa in Santurce

El Hormiguero (The Ant Colony) was a community social center in Santurce housed in a three-floor building on Avenida Fernandez Juncos near Parada 18.[1] It was occupied, organized, and defended by a diverse group of activists who took possession of the building on December 24, 2016, for about three years. I joined the project in October 2016 when a close friend connected me to the initiative. Hearing my own interest in securing a space for my own burgeoning lifework amid frustration at the rapid gentrification of the city, he suggested I join this effort to occupy.

El Hormiguero was imagined as a response to the debt crisis. This group wanted to take a stand against the rapid gentrification of the city and the outmigration of hundreds of thousands of Puerto Ricans. We wanted to lead a politicized squatting movement on the island, encouraging others to take over buildings and to retake the city. We imagined spaces where organizers and collectives working for a just recovery could freely gather, to live and dream together. Little did we know that after Hurricane Maria, occupying would become one of the major ways that communities would organize to reclaim spaces.

In this microhistory of the occupation, I provide an overview of the project and offer my perspective on the internal challenges we faced in sharing power. I hope these reflections will resonate with those who have also participated in horizontally organized movement spaces. I close by offering reflections on the potential challenges we encounter in creating spaces where all people belong.

The first proposal for El Hormiguero was drawn up and presented to Jornada Se acabaron Las Promesas (The promises are over) by Abner Dennis and Pamela Morales. It was not taken up by the group, in part because it represented a different approach to change work than that used by the direct-action group to mobilize. A few people expressed interest in joining the initiative, and El Hormiguero grew slowly by word of mouth.

Abner and Pamela's vision was to encourage a series of occupations to slow the privatization of the city and make visible the actors who were responsible for leaving the city in a state of abandonment. They believed that each occupation could provide a space for radical, leftist organizers to meet and build with people who lived in the communities where the occupations were organized. Hopefully, this would expand the size of our social movements. The organizers understood that efforts to build power and expand our networks had to involve everyday folks not already part of movement work to truly scale up, something they felt was necessary to fight the debt.

The early months of the group's founding were filled with an intensive research process. We consulted with attorneys about the legal ramifications of an occupation and studied prior cases of successful takeovers of buildings like that of Casa Taft 169. Casa Taft had been abandoned for about forty years before it was occupied by a small group of residents from the Machuchal community in Santurce. They transformed the property into a civic center and have secured several large grants to turn it into an off-grid community space. This case, while extremely unique, also spoke to a possibility that we longed for: to be able to turn the abandonment into something positive for the residents themselves.

We also faced multiple barriers to creating a movement on these terms. First, the length of time required for a person to occupy a property is so long that it's basically impossible to establish a claim for ownership.[2] We knew that our best chance was to find a building in debt to the city or whose owner had died and had no children interested in taking possession of the building.[3] One of the members of the collective worked for the city and got us access to a citywide list of buildings in "dis-use," an ambiguous government name for a building that had been abandoned by its owners.

We followed a maze of documents to locate owners of buildings we were interested in. In Puerto Rico all properties are traceable by *número de finca,* a unique nonsequential number that each property is linked to at the time of its formal recognition. Without this number it is impossible to trace ownership. Although the government did create an online map to make identifying the property number a bit easier, it was not reliable. On occasion we went through pages and pages of handwritten notes in El Registro de Propiedades (The Property Registry) to find the data we needed.

As we conducted the research on ownership and debt, we also made scouting trips to visit the buildings that were most promising. We decided to not occupy any building that already had inhabitants. Many apparently "abandoned" buildings in the city are home to the large houseless population in the city so we decided it was unethical to push others out. During this time we also conducted an analysis of the physical structures itself. Pamela created a checklist for each of us to carry as we walked through buildings doing our best to surmise the building's condition. If any building passed through the initial stages, we then had to analyze the likelihood that a building we took over would remain uncontested.

Those three months of research were gloriously exciting times. The core was small yet deeply committed. Together we researched title, debts, and conditions of over thirty buildings before choosing the one to be occupied. Our meetings danced between planning, visioning, and sharing our own stories. Before settling on a name or on a building, we wrote principles of our occupation collectively, first by selecting a few terms that we resonated with.[4] Each of us had time to write a reflection about the terms on their own, and then we put these definitions together, as in a story or jigsaw puzzle.

We looked after each other. I remember others making calls and texts to check on me when I missed a meeting. I remember feeling uplifted and seen. But, as we got closer and closer to the actual occupation, there was a marked shift in the content of meetings as well as the pace. Some were anxious to get to the "real work" of occupying a building while a smaller group protested. Because my own interests are in supporting internal reflection and healing in community, I was one of the those in the smaller group that wanted to slow down. I remember one meeting early on where I drew attention to the lack of focus on our own process, on finalizing our principles, setting protocols, and discussing *how* we build together. As a group, we decided to rotate our biweekly meetings between theory and practice, by spending half our time attending to tasks related to process and the other half moving tasks related to the practicalities of the occupation.

At first, this worked. But eventually we reverted to another rhythm, in part because we didn't have a protocol for remaining accountable to the agreements made in prior meetings. There were a few (mostly, but not exclusively) male voices who dominated conversations, and only a handful of people were responsible for planning and facilitating the meetings. Meeting agendas were jam-packed with heavy topics that contributed to a feeling of being stifled, and the general attitude was to push through. Only those with the most stamina had any say.

One day the group opted to eliminate quorum for making decisions. Again a few voices pushed for the change at a meeting that was poorly attended. The dominant voices said it was simply not feasible to keep on waiting for others to make decisions citing lack of agility and that not all members were equally committed. The logic was that if we had to wait around for others who were not coming to meetings to make decisions, we would never move forward on the project. It was a tense meeting, and ultimately the proposal to end quorum was successful. Nothing else was put in place to continue to maintain balance and agreement among the group.

After that, unofficial power plays became the norm because there was no process for aligning our values with our actions and things kept spiraling out of control. I found myself exhausted at the end of meetings. How could this be a real alternative to capitalist logics of extraction, expendability, and efficiency if I was so wiped out? I resorted to complaining and strategizing with others outside meetings. There were about five of us, all femme identified who felt there was a male dominance in the group. But these venting sessions didn't help; to the contrary it just got harder to speak my mind at meetings.

Things got worse after we found the building to occupy. It was a three-floor office space that had been abandoned about eight years earlier by Comunidades al Día, a community assistance program created during the Jorge Santini Administration. We liked the idea of taking back a building that neighbors remembered as a place they could get resources. When we went to scout the building, one of the members of the collective who climbed inside reported that it had been left with filing cabinets full of paperwork. There were remnants of Christmas party decorations still hanging from the ceiling as if the government just abandoned it after the holidays. No one lived there. The owner was still alive, and the building only had a medium-sized debt attached to it. While not ideal, we decided it was good enough for a first try.

The day the group "selected" for the occupation (December 24, 2016) is a good example of subtle power plays that reflected a lack of horizontality that began to dominate our process. We had just finished meeting for more than six hours and everyone was tired. As usual we had not covered everything and yet there was a pressing tension to discuss when the building would be occupied. Someone proposed Christmas Eve, a date that would not work for at least half of the group who had familial obligations. But a few were persistent. They downplayed the importance of the takeover saying, "We'll just be changing the locks." I think it was a combination of exhaustion and their persistence that led us to all finally "agree." It didn't feel like a collective process; it felt like giving in.

I had plans to visit my family in New York so I could not attend the takeover. As an anthropologist I know the deep significance of a ritual like "changing locks" and declaring a building ours. From that moment on I didn't feel truly a part of the group. But I stubbornly held on, adding tension to the group dynamic. I projected anger that could be sensed but not named directly.

The collective started to organize weekly brigades on Sundays to clean up the building. It was a massive undertaking, and the clean-up took eight months. From January to August 2017, the building was not opened to the public. The cofounder and leader, Abner, reflected on the date: "If I could do it differently, I would have just started with one floor and opened the building up right away." He recognized that it was difficult to maintain pace and motivation for such a long prelaunch period, even among the most dedicated.

As we began to focus more on the details of the management of the building, some started to become hyperconcerned with making things "efficient." Building relationships became secondary to cleaning up the building. I felt that many judged me for not participating in the brigades, but I found it hard to give my energy to something that did not truly have the space for my full self to show up. It felt like others hoped I'd just disappear, which made me hang on more stubbornly.

Participation became divided between those who attended meetings and those who came to clean and work on the rehabilitation of the space. Many were callous toward those who were not working on the cleanup, judging them for their lack of commitment. These attitudes slowly began to erode the quality of our relationships to each other and to the work. Rather than recognizing the powerful differential access we have to time, ability, and the different skillsets each person brought, one's value was directly proportionate to how much they could "contribute."

I stopped receiving texts or calls when I didn't turn up. When I did attend brigades, no one asked about my own life. It became clear that the building would not be home to multiple projects but would be the home of our collective. Any other projects wanting to use the space could only do so if they paid some contribution to El Hormiguero. We discussed ways to contract out space and forms of in-kind exchange that could be given in lieu of hard currency. It felt to me as if the space was becoming everyday more exclusive.

The group continued to grow. I found myself hurt all the time, struggling to heal the wounds. After many efforts to organize a meeting where I could interview the core members about the process, one comrade, Keila, helped me to organize a gathering that I described as an interview session in her house. It was held the night before Hurricane Maria was set to hit the island.

Instead of it being the place I hoped we could talk about our differences and reflect on our process, everyone got drunk and anxiously discussed the upcoming storm. I struggled to bring the group to the interview topics but there was so much anticipation in the space that it was hard to sustain. Only one of the four members I hoped to confront showed up. When Pamela finally arrived, she attacked me, asking where was my commitment? I felt the energy draining out from me again. It felt like a dead end.

Realistically, when the group stopped meeting my needs, I probably should have just left. Inhabiting this half-in, half-out space was not good for me or the group. Spending time on this kept me from more rewarding endeavors and seriously damaged my sense of well-being.

Post-Maria Note

The building had only been open about a month when Hurricane Maria hit. At first it felt like a new start. The space served as a point of contact for us without phone signal or internet. There was a definite focus on our relationships as we shared how each one had fared, supporting one another in the best way we could.

We also began to cultivate a relationship between some organizers in the neighboring community (Barriada Figueroa) and the okupa members. We organized brigades and facilitated donations. In part this was a response to the hurricane. El Hormiguero was one of the organizations that was participating in El Llamado and helped to get resources that were needed to its neighboring community. Hurricane Maria prompted a conversation about what it would take to really begin rehabilitating the space for living and not just as a social center. The group undertook brigades, finalizing and improving its rainwater catchment system, and setting up a solar system, and a few of the members of the collective moved in.

The energy I had to participate did not last, but it felt good to contribute. I watched from afar as the group transformed the building into a living okupa. Most people were paying rent for homes that didn't have water or electricity. It was even unclear when those services would be restored.

El Hormiguero's calendar of activities included an impressive lineup of diverse activities, including study circles and a personal defense group training karate. It also opened the space to other groups like the University Without Borders (Universidad Sin Fronteras) who taught a four-week class on collective leadership, and an artist's collective, Colectivo Columpio, began to use the space to train.

After close to six months had passed, I was invited to participate in a health clinic titled Sanación Solidaria (Solidarity Healing) organized by some new members. Excited to meet new members who were carrying out our earlier dream of using the social center for collective healing work, we agreed to participate. My partner and I designed an interactive station lesson on self-love.

No one engaged directly what we had made. Some visitors to the space took photos of each of the reflection stations, perhaps to do the work elsewhere, sensing this was not a safe space. There were no outbursts, just a lot of silence and surface conversations. I could feel the tension beneath the good graces. I tried to keep it positive. But the body does not lie. When I got home, I was so exhausted that I just collapsed. I could barely keep myself upright.

I completely disconnected from the group after this event. Later, I heard of allegations of gender-based violence occurring within the okupa. It was not clear if anything happened to bring accountability to the situation.

Soon after the violences that occurred internally, the owner showed up and began to assert his claim to the building. Within a few short months, members of El Hormiguero were evicted and the social center closed. The group gave away the possessions that had been donated and disbanded.

El Hormiguero brought me into direct contact with several challenges that are not unique but are notoriously difficult to address in horizontal collective organizing efforts. Relationships matter everywhere, but when we are trying to be egalitarian, it's essential. Since I didn't speak directly with the person I had an issue with, it fomented an air of mistrust. I learned that anytime we vent, gossip, or talk about what hurts without including the actual person in the conversation, we dilute the power of the collective. Critique is important to growth. We must compassionately bring it to the center. If I had done this, I would have had an informed decision about whether the group was the right place for me.

Although we long for horizontal, equitable relationships, it's important to remember that we are human, and we are all unlearning. In El Hormiguero, we changed the way decisions were made (dropping the need for quorum) without the full participation of everyone in the group. Take time at the start of a collective endeavor to dialogue the ways in which your group makes decisions and stick to it unless everyone agrees to shift.

Consensus is not perfect either. The tendency to go along with the group can mean that sometimes consensus is achieved by force. I learned to be more curious about the ways we unintentionally recreate inequality in our movement spaces when we don't get specific about the details. Creating community agreements early on and deciding on a decision-making structure, key roles, and what happens when things fall apart can help us stay centered in our shared mission. Often, the way things play out are complex but, if we are aware, we might notice and name power imbalances as part of a commitment to courageous conversations.[5]

Given the stories I heard about sexual violence that occurred later in the space, I am saddened that I was not able to shape change in another direction. Even as I notice myself assuming a degree of responsibility for what transpired in the space, I am learning to take things less personally. Transforming conflict is not easy but it is vital that we find ways to do so to create a space where we can all be free.

Lastly, when we want our work to be intentionally connecting different communities, we must bring that into the center from the beginning. El Hormiguero had a grand vision to join community (i.e., neighbors who were not formally organized) and a general activist community. That didn't really begin to happen until after Hurricane Maria. I imagine that working directly with the people from the surrounding barrios earlier on in the occupation would have changed the pace and focus of our endeavor. But this is exactly the point.

El Llamado

Sustaining Movements over the Long Haul

El Llamado (The Calling) was imagined as a movement support center by Xiomara Caro. She dreamed it up in response to her own experiences as a student organizer and later as a capacity builder and funder of social justice movements across the archipelago. After playing a leadership role in the 2010 University of Puerto Rico system wide strike, Xiomara, like many others, graduated and never processed what happened. She found herself thrown into a full-time job, organizing afterhours and offering support to many groups opposing the debt crisis. She felt exhausted. Eventually she realized the problem was in the things left unsaid and how folks were organizing. A culture of well-being was absent. She longed for a movement space that could hold these emotions and create space for healing. Like Spenta Kandawalla of Generative Somatics, she knew that "both [healing and organizing] are necessary—for our well-being and to build power together, to shift conditions and to live with more freedom."[1] El Llamado was imagined as a physical hub where organizers could be supported in their transformations as people dedicated to change.

Over the span of one year, Xiomara launched two versions of El Llamado, each operating as a pilot, clarifying key challenges and possibilities for bridging healing and social justice. Each of these spaces—a regular meeting group of activists from across a wide range of leftist organizations and a post-Maria movement support space—provide important insights into the challenges that arise when we strive to create a culture shift. El Llamado gave me firsthand experience of the role of our emotions in our organizing, the power of community agreements, and the challenge of taking an individual dream and making it into a collective project. I am eternally grateful for this space and for

Xiomara's leadership, which helped me follow my calling, take on new shapes (roles), and trust my own offerings. In what follows, I offer a trajectory and analysis of each of these spaces in the hopes that it will support the project's rebirth.

First Pilot: La Huelga 2016

It took six years for a strong student organization to mobilize another massive strike in the UPR system after the 2010 systemwide strike. But by 2016, new organizers at the public university were going after national actors. They demanded that the public debt be audited and denounced the role of the Fiscal Control Board. After all, it was la junta's proposed $450 million cut to the already fledging university budget that had activated the mobilization. Xiomara explained it to me as such: "They were much more ambitious and audacious than we were as they were raising national claims against the debt and PROMESA." At the same time, she and other organized were concerned. These new strikers were bold, but could they really build a strategy to win? Most of these students had never participated in a direct action, let alone organized a takeover of a school. And so the first pilot for El Llamado was born.

Xiomara wrote to organizers, artists, and researchers, inviting us to join her in cocreating a holistic model of support for these youth organizers. Her proposal asked each person to form a part of one of four committees: research, communications, organizing/political strategy, and well-being. The objective of the first group was to help the students gather and organize information about the debt so that they could be used in campaigns. The research produced in the first committee would be used for communications with the public. The communications committee would help organizers design educational materials aimed at intervening in the public narrative, largely controlled by big banks, business, and government. The organizing committee was charged with developing students' capacity to grow the mobilization through active recruitment. The well-being committee was composed of people who specialized in movement, yoga, meditation, dance, music, and other practices that facilitate healing. Through an array of healing arts, organizers would discover practices that could be integrated into their movement processes, transforming the spaces of struggle by transforming the people in them.

At the first meeting the group collectively decided well-being should not be its own committee. Instead, we thought that it should be a circle enveloping the other committees, a through line present in each. By including mind, body, and spirit in the idea of leadership development, the group was together committed to integrating art, culture, and healing into the design, execution, and group process. It sounded like a good idea in theory, but something else happened in practice.

Only a few people were directly involved with the students' efforts. Trainings were organized through El Llamado, which many of us participated in with some key student leaders. They included topics like how to run a campaign, get clear on one's vision and purpose, how to develop campaign materials, and how to conduct a power mapping. A group of older activists began meeting together weekly for their own well-being.

The meetings were a breath of fresh air, a place to process the news and the old traumas from the 2010 movement suddenly made very real again for those of us witnessing the students organize in the present. Our gatherings followed the "agile learning methodology," offered by Alex Aldarondo who is a facilitator and at the time, ran an afterschool program based on the method. We used the methodology to design meetings.[2]

At the start of each meeting we decided the terms of engagement. By moving a few chips on a board, we set the parameters: how long we would meet, speaking order, how to sit, and the purpose of our gathering. True to its goals of speed, flexibility, and collaboration, our meetings were very generative. Because we cocreated the container together, we finished most meetings on time or early. We made time for emotions—connecting with check-ins and check-outs, as well as all kinds of games. Each member was given space to try out their dream projects and share our own personal "calling" with the group.

More than anything else, a space was created for activists who were no longer students to process lingering issues from their time as strikers and to share their reflections about the new mobilization they were witnessing. One of the difficulties then was that few participants of El Llamado were currently in an organizing role. Even if they were organizing as part of a union or other structure, few were doing so as part of the student strike. In addition, the few members of El Llamado who were offering direct support to the students did not regularly attend meetings.

Arguably then, the meeting space was easily "balanced" without the stressful pressure constraints characteristic of an ongoing mobilization against a specific target. Other collectives and organizations critiqued the effort, arguing that it "took activists away" from their other commitments and those doing "real work." The idea was that it was diluting movement capacity rather than building it. This is a division that I have seen play out again and again. Locally, there is still a very strong repulsion to anything related to "self-care" and there's not a very clear integration of healing into our traditional movement spaces; it stays peripheral.

Part of the criticisms could have been avoided by making joining the group more effortless. In fact, El Llamado was not public since we convened as a behind-the-scenes support group. In the beginning, it made sense to keep our identity secret. But as our reality evolved, this secrecy created a dynamic where we never felt comfortable inviting anyone who hadn't already been invited by Xiomara to attend meetings. I think we may have become very protective of this space, which kept it small. El Llamado was a space we were invited to be our full selves. It was a space that we went to feel held, to hide out and debrief after large-scale manifestations. It was a home.

People shared their deepest longings in this space. I first learned about Pueblo Crítico, a project birthed by social worker Kamil Gerónimo-López to foment critical thinking through board games and popular education more broadly with people who do not actively organize or who may not have formal schooling. I loved how student organizer González-Sampayo used La Oasis (the name of our meeting space) to host an encounter with other student organizers that challenged internal dynamics of callout culture in the student movement. I led grounding exercises for the first time in Puerto Rico in this space.

While each of us was welcome, most people did not take center stage. There was a collective appreciation for Xiomara herself that bordered on unhealthy obsession. I noticed that this adoration made it hard for the group to become horizontal in practice because everyone was looking to Xiomara for direction.

For example, Xiomara traveled a lot. One day, after giving a small presentation on the vision of the project, she left a group of us to work through the materials she created and to start formalizing the structure. In our meeting, without the anchor of Xiomara, it was difficult to find momentum. Many did not dare to make decisions without consulting with her, so little was achieved.

I continued in the steering committee until the group secured funding to develop a leadership pilot for students in moments of transition. This included both the transitional moment between two organizing campaigns as well as those who had just graduated from university. Now charged with implementation of a grant, the energy of meetings shifted. It felt restricted and became much more familiar to the kinds of gatherings I participated in other movement spaces. I didn't know how to transform what I was witnessing but I knew that I didn't want to execute a vision I didn't help to shape. I wanted to play a bigger role in deciding what we were to build, so I withdrew my participation. My decision was respected, and I was immediately taken off certain emails and group chats. I felt a mix of frustration and pleasure. I had, after all, not made the same mistake as I had in El Hormiguero. Seeing a lack of alignment between theory and practice, I made my way "out" without burning bridges. But I didn't find a way to turn my discomfort into a change for the whole group, still a deep longing for me.

In later conversations, Xiomara admitted that the whole thing felt like a runaway train. She wasn't feeling in alignment either and was unsure if she wanted El Llamado to be sponsored by a larger US-based organization. She wasn't feeling excited but rather trapped by the plans she had made. They were planning to go public and launch programming, when suddenly Hurricane Maria hit and another version of El Llamado was born. This time as an emergency response and movement meeting center.

Second Pilot: Meeting Ground for Mutual Aid and Just Ricanstruction

After the storm, one of El Llamado's members, Luis Calderon, offered his business Cucina 135—a commercial kitchen with a small patio in the middle of the city—as a place for us to meet and organize mutual aid. At Cucina, nearly twenty collectives and grassroots organizations convened regularly to share stories, challenges, and needs of their specific communities. We had access to a hot lunch, filtered water, the internet through hotspots, and a landline to make and receive calls. We also had access to solar-panel chargers to charge our phones. All this was provided through the generous donations that arrived through Xiomara's employer (Center for Popular Democracy) and the nascent Maria Fund. Given that nearly 100 percent of the island was living without electricity, these material gifts provided undeniable sustenance. We were given resources for what we needed so that we could continue to do the work.

Initially we met daily, but this rhythm became more intermittent over the two months' time we were there. In daily meetings, we set priorities for the day. The organizing team was divided into committees:

those working on communications—on contesting the mainstream media story about the hurricane relief efforts—and work brigades led by those who were going to communities to help reconstruction efforts. Although the major focus was on getting supplies to key organizations and communities in need, there was an intention to build a culture of well-being in the space.

In the context of blackout, being connected kept feelings of help-lessness and powerlessness at bay. We were facing mass insecurity, but hearing what other groups were doing helped us to feel inspired. It reas-sured us that we were doing all we could. At least we were not alone. Meeting and planning together was one way to overcome isolation. As we realized our essential connection to others, we discovered our true nature as part of an interconnected web of life.

Despite the intention we shared to center our well-being as we responded to the crisis, there was an undeniably intense rhythm that dominated El Llamado. We received a constant stream of media folks from established channels and independent projects as diverse as MTV, Al Jazeera, Defend Puerto Rico, and teleSUR. The kitchen was covered in big sticky notes from the previous meetings, with talking points that directly addressed media claims, priorities for the day, and announcements.

Despite all the joys and possibilities won in this space of encoun-ters, I noticed Xiomara and other key organizers of the space gaunt, exhaustion palpable on their faces. Deeply immersed in the pace of organizing, this second pilot lacked the feeling of balance and support the first pilot had. That's not to say that the space wasn't given. But the healing circles I co-organized were mostly attended by those who came to the space seeking community but did not hold specific roles in leadership. I still remember the first weekly healing circle we offered. Fifteen minutes into our start time, everything continued in a normal frantic rhythm inside though a small circle had begun to form on the patio outside. I stepped into the main building and invited everyone to take a break and come out to join us. There was an awkward pause, a few apologized but no one came.

Post-Maria Note

Suddenly, it ended. The decision was informed in part by the changing conditions. Slowly, things began to feel more "normal." Phone signals got better. Electricity was reestablished across most of the main island

of the archipelago. Many went back to work. But it was also exhaust-
ing to keep the meeting space open for twelve to fourteen hours a day.
Xiomara explained the decision in those terms. "I came in [after a trip]
and saw my team very de-motivated and frustrated. No one else was
there. I said, that's it. It's over. It ends now." Once the space closed, we
couldn't really pick back up either version of El Llamado again, though
we tried at the six-month mark to meet again.

It's unclear what El Llamado will become in the future. Currently, El
Llamado is inactive or, as I like to think of it, incubating in the dark. I
continue to believe deeply in this project. It's one I hope to continue to
flock, whatever name it ends up with. I know others feel this way too.
El Llamado is a calling to be whole people healing in our moves toward
liberation. To me this is one of the first biggest successes of the initiative. I'm hopeful it will again come alive in the future.

Sprouting Ancestral Futures
CEPA's Healing Justice Practice

The Center for Embodied Pedagogy and Action (CEPA) is an organization that I founded in 2016, which began as an effort to reimagine my work beyond the university. It was based on the notion that for learning to be transformative, we are charged with embodying what we seek to teach and taking appropriate action. I was following a yearning as a person born and raised in the diaspora to return to my homeland and contribute to its liberation.

Today, CEPA has evolved into a healing justice project centering queer folx, often women, nonbinary, and trans folx committed to fostering the decolonization of Puerto Rico through initiatives that support our individual and collective capacity to live in wholeness. Centering the leadership of those who have been marginalized and oppressed under patriarchy is vital to cultivating a decolonial present. The project is led by myself and my partner in love and life, Lau Pat RA. Lau was born, raised, and educated in Boriké and is a visual artist, healer, and visionary. This microhistory was nourished by a series of dialogues I had with Lau in 2021 and personal reflections on living and working in Boriké for the last six years.

When Guabancex (Hurricane Maria) blew through the island archipelago, Lau and I began to collaborate actively. Each of our disciplinary trainings as anthropologist and visual artist merged to craft a spiritually and politically grounded form of healing. We saw that the hurricane revealed the psychological, physical, and spiritual legacies of colonialism and wanted to offer tools to move through what folks were facing while offering beauty and a space to rest and to dream. With the support of Adela Nieves and Eroc Arroyo-Montano—two Boricua healers based in the diaspora—we began to develop wellness kits to be distributed on the work brigades being organized out of El Llamado.[1] Lau crafted a prototype for the kit with recycled boxes and even made a xylography design of our logo. The kits were always unique but often included tinctures, teas, salves, solidarity love notes, and educational graphics to help people process trauma and other conditions rampant at the time (e.g., insomnia, pain, overwhelm, and low immunity). We also held weekly healing circles with those on the frontlines of rebuilding efforts. For three months, we facilitated weekly spaces to anyone facing over-whelm, though we most often worked with organizers and caregivers. In the spaces, we offered simple techniques for grounding, processing, and releasing the difficult emotions that had come to the surface in the immediate aftermath of Hurricane Maria. In the calm that came after, we invited folks to dream around the central question: how does one decolonize in mind, body, and spirit?

Once things began to stabilize after the storm's passage, we found ourselves a home base in Río Piedras and have been living and working in a *casa-taller* (home-workshop) since then. The *casa-taller* is now the base of operations for CEPA; it is where we ground vision for decolo-nizing our daily life. The space is anchored by over seventy medicinal plants and foods planted in our yard and our driveway. There are collec-tive spaces for working, creating, and practicing together.

We also designed and have been running a visitor solidarity program targeting other queer diaspora-based Boricuas and close allies from Black, Latinx, and Indigenous communities. Many of the people who have visited are themselves second- or third-generation Puerto Ricans who have not been able to connect to the archipelago because of lan-guage barriers or disconnection from their family due to discrimination or outright refusal to accept diverse forms of gender and sexual identi-ties. We are dedicated to practicing decolonizing this world, beginning with the way our social and economic identities are created and sus-tained at "home." Over time we came to realize that through the visitor solidarity program we were cultivating a small-scale solidarity economy and transnational network.

We see the visitor solidarity program as a practice space for what is to come, as well as a place that breaks with the isolation the system tries to impose on us. The program operates on a sliding scale to ensure that as many people who want to participate can regardless of their financial circumstances. This work has been very difficult at times, but we are learning to speak more openly about money and privilege and sharing in a way that has closed the gap between our values and actions. We have received feedback that, despite the location of our *casa-taller* in the middle of the city, the space itself feels peaceful, surrounded by plant allies, ancestors, and community.

Beyond the work we have done to tend this small patch of land, we also cocreate practice spaces for groups. These circles usually include some form of rest, breathwork, creative exploration, and processing. We have experimented with ways to democratize traditional healing methods from the Caribbean and to guide others in their healing process. We have developed zines, curricula, and manuals. In 2019 CEPA was commissioned by Florida-based nonprofit Organize Florida to develop a curriculum called "Decolonizing for Organizers." Realizing the mammoth task ahead of us, we sought out others to cocreate the content. We wound up working with three others: Adela Nieves, Olatokunboh Obasi, and Pao Lebron. We were inspired by the Taino medicine wheel to offer instruction on how to shift from the hero-centric model of organizing into an integrative practice of decolonizing informed by the medicine of the elements: earth, water, fire, and air. During the pandemic, we used this curriculum as a baseline to craft a six-month learning and healing experience for BIPOC. There were seven pods based in different lands colonized by the United States and our collective study was centered on landback and reparations.

As a result of our work to sustain healing space, we have also found ourselves serving as guides for others in our queer community and in the larger social movement ecosystem in Boriké who need support to move through conflict. We are only beginning this work now but see that it is a vital component of building worlds that are not replicas of the systems we seek to dismantle. We have responded as our capacity allows to ground us in our collective strength and health. Our goal is to midwife new ways of caring for each other as we compost systems of harm and abuse. Within our organization, we have prioritized building internal cultures of care that support us in practicing this at the most intimate level.

The central axis of our work is healing justice, which is by nature an intersectional practice of untangling our essence from the roots of oppression so we can live in freedom. We are very much interested in the most intimate sphere of healing: relationships. We begin with our bodies, our own personal earth. Through healing, we can regain a sense of belonging to the earth and all other life, be they people, other species, or the elements themselves.

In Puerto Rico healing justice is inseparable from decolonization. Lau explains the connection between these two terms:

> The religious fanaticism that exists in Puerto Rico is an element of our society that entraps us. It is powerful to claim our spirituality outside of that, to feel that we innately have access to healing and experiencing pleasure and health. The church tells us that we have to depend on another person to save us and that we must surrender our will to him. Everything in this worldview supports the idea that power is always outside us. So to be able to feel our agency to be self-determining from the food we eat to the emotions we feel is truly radical.[2]

Lau's words reflect the fact that our decolonization is dependent on our ability to remember, reclaim, and practice our spiritual traditions that the church wanted to eradicate. It means that we claim our sovereignty and embody the knowing that this is inherent to our being, rather than something that we win or lose based on where we sit in society.

Part of the walk home on this journey has also meant reclaiming ancestral traditions. In Puerto Rico, where both the indigenous and African are relegated to the past, we believe that actively cultivating our Afro-Indigenous practices is essential. Thanks to the elders of Tribu Yuké based in Jayuya, we have begun the path of remembering by connecting with the elements and our ancestors.

At times it has felt like a very long walk home. The legacy of binary thinking inherited by colonialism has meant that elders also are unlearning and can sometimes simplify the dualistic forces of energies inherent to all life. For example, instead of our bateyes being spaces to anchor the divine masculine or feminine, they are called the "woman's batey" or "man's batey."[3]

We are committed to offering support to our Taino elders in learning language justice and honoring the role of queer and nonbinary, trans, and two-spirit people in healing. Lau adds, "That's why . . . healing justice is about honoring all of life. Without waiting for someone else to come in and give that connection back to you." This diverse weaving is part of our function and commitment to decolonize. The queer approach to decolonizing means that we are in a constant becoming, a transformation without end.[4]

Delimiting or specializing in the work of decolonizing can be difficult. As we pull back the layers, we find further to go. It took close to five years before we even started to develop a vision for how the world would look if we were to "win" on this journey. To ensure that our work does not fall into the trap of mere metaphor, we have always been clear that returning lands and stewardship to Indigenous peoples is vital.[5] The landback movement is complicated by the continued erasure of indigeneity in Boriké. There are no federally recognized tribes or nations; even within the social movement ecology locally, folks adhere to the myth that all Indigenous peoples were exterminated during colonialism. Today, all our most precious natural resources are property of the US government.

We are ourselves in the process of reclaiming our indigeneity, and our elders also began that reclamation journey over thirty years ago. Facing this complexity, we want to imagine other possibilities for being in relationship with this archipelago. We believe that by healing our mental, spiritual, social, and emotional relations, we can encourage a culture shift that will prepare us for the massive transformation that decolonization requires of the world as it is currently set up. Part of the groundwork is in the healing of the interpersonal violence imprinted on us and reproduced by us in society.

Since Lau and I are also in a romantic relationship, this is work that goes deep. It asks us to examine and actively work with our own traumas. For example, we are learning how to keep a boundary around work and life, which is challenging since everything occurs in the same place with the same people. I (Melissa) personally tend toward the overwork, which puts a drain on my relationships. I am grateful to Lau for helping me to open to the transformations. Lau agreed. "We are reparenting one another. It's made me conscious, and I've witnessed changes in you and myself. As a result, I know myself better and I am learning how to stay in my center and to be able to walk in integrity in all parts of my life."

Together we have a shared commitment to unlearning and showing up in new ways. The ways we have been taught to partner don't fit within our current vision of a life lived joyfully. Even as we affirm our work as caregivers and healers, we are also working to give back to ourselves so that we are not falling into the pattern of always giving first to others and leaving ourselves for last. I really think we are reconnecting with our own power individually and creating a romantic relationship that supports this turning inward to grow beyond pain, stress, and trauma.

For the last two years we have grown our core leadership collective to eight people, making it more possible to go at a pace that is joyful even as it is heavy. Recognizing that land stewardship would be impossible without a sense of security and safe place to call home, in 2023 we purchased the *casa-taller* in a seller-financed sale. With a lot of help from community, hours of fundraising and persistence, we have secured a home for CEPA.

In many ways, CEPA is just at the start of its journey. We want to create networks of sustainability all over the Caribbean as our ancestors did. We want to build indigiqueer palenques where we can go deeper into our efforts to steward this beautiful earth and to live our life in ceremony.[6] We have reached a place in our work where it feels vital to build closer to home, within the Caribbean. We want to leave something intact for future generations, as a land trust or collective ownership model or something we still do not have a name for. Facing mass displacement, we realize the importance of cultivating collective places for Boricuas to (return and) stay. We imagine these palenques as a place for those who were born and raised on the island and those who have returned to build sanctuary and a home together.

Embodying Freedom, a Praise Song

Freedom is a practice. It is a revealing within the self. The molten core or creative spark becomes matter. It remembers the passion in simple abundance. Then it undulates outward, becoming expression—a truth or essence—before finally becoming community. Freedom's dance is not linear but a spiral movement. Relating, unlearning, healing, and occupying are core practices on this journey. They are the medicine and the path for liberation. I sing their praises, hum through difficulties, and stay for the trouble.

Relating

Decolonizing is always about relating. Not only to others. Often, the deepest work is in coming to terms with all the parts of yourself. It is holding the light and the shadow with equal reverence. Memories may be dark, may be triggering AF or a gaping hole of nothing. Yet, they are with you. And are necessary to remember if you want to claim freedom. Relating is also about the earth. It asks, do you see the land as kin? Do you recognize the abundant gifts that come from the land? Do you know any allies from the plant and mineral world? Decolonizing begins by sensing the relations that sustain you, then offering them gratitude and love. Indigenizing is humbler still. Understanding that what you believe you are sensing is first noticing you.

The baseline of building alternatives lives in relation. Relating differently is only possible if you operate with the knowing that colonial logics designed "self and other" and "center and margin" as ways to justify pillage, destruction, and separation.

How can I remember that conflict can be solved with more love? How can I enact that love without swallowing more trauma? How do I know my right size after centuries of shrinking and hiding to fit? To pass? To survive?

Relating is a process. For me it has begun with an effort to trust the body to tell me what I need to know. I read the quickening of my heartbeat as a sign that I need to speak my truth. I trust discomfort as a place to stay, evidence that a path to growth has just entered the edge of my awareness.

To constantly improve and grow relationally, you have to get curious about what happens when you relate, and it fails just as much as when connection blossoms. You must remember that everyone you meet is a teacher, reflecting back something about you that you may not want to see about yourself. I say you, but I'm really talking about me.

I find the Mayan phrase "In Lak'ech Ala K'in" one day in the pages of a philosophy article critiquing Enrique Dussel.[1] *Tu eres mi otro yo* (You are my other me). This indigenous epistemology continues to unravel me each time I hear it. It speaks to a fundamental truth: we are forever interdependent beings. To know that you are in a different body, with a different experience, and a different relationship to privilege and oppression is one thing. To be free of the myth of individualism and act in accordance with this spiritual code is quite another. But embodying a different pathway to liberation that recognizes our sameness takes a lot more than knowing. It takes deep internal work to really relate. If we can't build with each other, it doesn't matter what skills we have. They will never add up and we will remain lost in separation.

As a person from the diaspora, language has been a barrier to relating. I constantly remind myself that both English and Spanish are colonial languages even as I learn to speak Spanish to make community in Boriké. Here I am remembering how to speak to you. I only leave for ten days, but I return with Spanish staccato, slow and stagnant. "I noticed you've been making a lot more errors than usual," she says with affection. This is not news to me. I hear my grammatical mistakes belatedly, often a second after the words have become breath and sound, too late to do anything but cringe. I feel the walls climb rapidly between my tongue and thoughts as I question my competency and my inner critic takes hold. I furiously type and erase text messages, say everything fast, like mush. It all becomes a vicious cycle. Even though I know logically these gaps will close in time—they have before—the transformation is painful.

I marvel at those who feel at home in multiple languages. In me these languages battle for primacy unless they can share home as Spanglish. I remember though that mutual support can only come after I open to these truths. Relating requires vulnerability. I must help myself by becoming vulnerable to others, yielding and growing boundaries that are adaptable and firm as I develop the wisdom to know when to use which. Relating only works if I keep my attention on my part. Only then can I be a cocreator with the universe. Only then can I counter the dominant culture of isolation and self-sufficiency that keeps us from truly relating and transforming disconnection.

But relating is not just hard. It can also bring to life the gift of more possibilities. When we are in relationship, we realize how much more choice is available than our patterns and pain would have us believe. And the beauty of relationship is that we don't need to be the same size always. Some days I may pass stealth in the background, other days I may take center stage, and others still I might choose smallness.

So, always remember your power.

You. Me. We.

Together, we have a real chance of staying alive.

Unlearning

Unlearning requires honesty, openness, and willingness to change. I have had to take off the armor, soften the discipline and the fear ingrained in me by a strict momma, and all the rigidity that comes with thriving under the violence of "excellent" schooling. In Spanish, there are other words that get me closer to the feeling unlearning evokes in me. Words like *formarse* or *capacitarse*. Each describes learning as a molding or shaping. Even though capacity building is a term co-opted by nonprofits, the idea of "growing capacity" serves as a north star for me in my unlearning path. Capitalism would have us all believe there's not enough. But unlearning asks other questions. What is no longer true? What is not mine? What is enough?

When we are not one but many we can develop and strengthen as a collective by recognizing the diversity of skills, instincts, abilities, processes, and resources available. We know through firsthand experience that we already have everything we need.

Unlearning requires support to take root. Not all of it comes from within. We need others to witness us in our shapeshifting. We are social beings; we need to feel we belong. We need to learn together. The practice of shaping oneself is unending. In the movement away from the hierarchy that charismatic leadership fomented in liberation work, we began to call for leaderful groups. Of course, if there's only one carrying around a dream, it's easy to destroy.

I am learning how to reshape and unlearn my relationship to perfection. Sometimes that means I have to be brave enough to share my ideas freely. This means not only being vulnerable to others but also working to let go of the proprietary concept of "mine" when speaking of dreams. I find this not only challenging but also liberating. It means that I can tune into an intelligence and create a call but that it can only happen with others and collaboration with spirit. Not only does this way of thinking and acting take the pressure off, it's also more truthful. We are all in our own ways channeling the solutions to our times.

Are you open to taking on your part?

Gustavo (thinking with Ivan Illich) of La Universidad de la Tierra in Oaxaca explained the difference to me in this way. When we speak about "educating" others, we have already fallen for the trap that some of us "know," whereas others are ignorant. We have fallen for the trap that some of us have finished "learning" so we teach. But we always have more to learn and more to grow. Especially when we are talking about unlearning patterns of conquest. Understanding that first and foremost: Decolonizing is itself a process of unlearning intertwined with a laundry list of realities. Displacement. Devastation. Assimilation. Erasure.

Where will you begin? I don't know. But the best place, I've heard, is just where you are.

Today, I'm unlearning the soft, performative forms of solidarity and moving shifting into coliberation. I am unlearning an identity—a worldview principally made in the diaspora—toward a Caribbean, island one. This unlearning has less to do with my essence, and more to do with my openness to be shaped by the wisdom of my day-to-day experience in the geography of an archipelago and in my life in this region.

The sustained, ongoing commitment it takes to unlearn is tiring at times. But I know that each day, I am unlearning the myth of superiority bestowed upon me through private education. I am finding the parallels between how I live and what needs to be transformed.

Language continues to be a sharp edge for me in this transformation. I worked so hard to learn academic speak. But now I must bring down the barriers that jargon created in me speaking with my people in exchange for gaining access to "higher" education. It feels like taking down a wall and requires translating thought into heart and spirit. I must speak to the essence. Something I know these institutions wanted me to forget.

I am remembering how to speak to you. After all those years finding language for the things that plagued, paralyzed, and pulverized my sense of self-worth, I became utterly frustrated with my family. I had so little patience for them in my college years and I expressed it regularly, ready to deconstruct anything they said. "I should have never sent you to that school," mom says at one point when things reached a crescendo.

Now, later, cooled by time and maturity, I can see how that story was incomplete. It marked a losing of me, on the one hand—but also a coming into myself. Learning the outline of myself in those years was key to my survival. But now I want to go beyond an individualist notion of survival. And that requires talking to you again.

I feel defeat when other loved ones talk about my academic mark. You're so poetic (at best) or idealistic or incomprehensible (at worst). I know I'm still swimming in a pool of jargon. And yet I believe in the transformative power of language so I'm trying and trying to stretch the current limits of my imagination using strange words and moving instinctually.

Slow. Steady.

If every word has power folded into it, then I choose to work for decolonization because I think its basic, nay, foundational to transforming Boriké. The binaries we inherited from colonization impede us in all kinds of ways.

Today I'm unlearning the binary between scarcity and abundance. I wonder: how do we dissolve the financial world as it currently operates while also capturing a sense of real wealth for all marginalized people? I'm open to compromise with you on the best terms or, at least, get the dialogue started because I realize that the only way to thrive is to break the barriers between us, not build more.

Searching for the middle path in the muck of everyday life is hard work. I am growing used to the feeling of sticky skin, of dreaming big but finding what's workable within the constraints at hand. I am learning to love falling into the mud. I am learning to love looking again. I am learning to love staying. I am learning to love awaiting the revelations that come after the rain.

Healing

This all began innocently enough. I was long fascinated by social movements. When I began to study them, I realize I was looking for healing. I collected stories of winning. These fissures and breaks were medicine. At first I mistook them for a pathway to greater security inside the system but they were more like idea bombs, exploding the limits of what I thought was possible, changing my ideas of success and the meaning of a life well lived.

It's a funny thing, until you find the momentum to act, longing for something else can make you feel crazy. Angry. Dissatisfied with life. Wondering, is this really all there is? You go along with it, until something breaks. Because if we're honest, healing is simple but not easy.

Healing requires softening your attitude toward yourself. And mine is NYC mean. Today I try to find joy in the crazy. Read in it a sign that I'm paying attention, temporarily weighed down by the suffering in our world. But the visions are there too. Even though listening to them is frightening in my waking hours.

Do we dare pull out the root of our dis-ease(s)? What might it require to change our lives? How would it shift the stories we tell ourselves? Our own sense of responsibility? Half of life is deciding which contradictions to live with, my mentor Gina reminds me constantly.

As colonized peoples, we hold a lot of collective trauma today that we don't remember consciously. *It hurt too much to remember.* The poverty. The struggles. The hunger. The rejection. But here's the thing: what you don't remember consciously gets buried and it stays with you. You don't need to recuperate the memories to free yourself of the weight. You can release the inheritances. The debts. That's the good news. But you DO have to sit down, listen, and feel these unprocessed weights to release them from your system. Maybe that's the bad news.

If you are anything like me, you must mourn all that you will never recover. Your grief can be art, it can make sense if you let it. It can help you release the grief for the conversations you never thought to have with your elders while they were still around. Especially those who died young or remained silent until death. I try to show compassion for living elders who only remember the pain and not much else. I let myself believe there are other ways to know and change the past.

Our traumas (just like our healing) are nonlinear. They can become intrusive. Insistent. They need reminders that you are safe now. They require awareness. Support. Breath.

Triggers are everywhere. They look like impossible standards for "political clarity." They look like violence inside our movements, sexual assault in our communities, self-destructive behaviors, or addictions.

When I talk to people who farm, who return to their family's barrio to work, create, or organize, I remember that there's immense beauty in healing the polarity between the temporal and the eternal. I am now. I am here. This present moment is the only place I can be. But I am shaping futures and pasts every time I can rupture a familial pattern and embody my values in a direct and intentional way. Ancient wisdom of indigenous peoples say that when we heal something today, we heal seven generations forward and backward. As adrienne maree brown would say, small is all. What you do matters. As Octavia Butler would say, shape change.[2]

Healing hurts. It means holding the fragments of yourself with their jagged edges and dangers. It means accepting the shadow parts of yourself that are filled with shame. It requires that we ask with curiosity and openness, how do I participate in my own oppression?

When I remember sexual assault, or the gray sexual violations that occurred when I myself didn't give consent but didn't say no either it hurts. Was it them or me who said, "Lay there. Shut up. It's almost over now." I honestly can't remember. But being able to look at that past, through the eyes of self-forgiveness and compassion while feeling the impact of all the ways in which consent is given and broken is deep spiritual practice. Knowing how and when I tend to betray myself and how ingrained denouncing my own needs are begins my liberation from the ruts of self-denial.

To be whole, we must find the fragments of ourselves. Pick them up. Dust them off. Call them in. Integrate them.

Buddhist texts call suffering the nature of human existence. The task of this existence for them is to learn how to leave suffering behind. To inhabit a middle point between reaction and presence. We suffer because we cling. Wanting things to never change. We suffer because we want to be in the comfort of what is known. The comfort of the past. Even if its funky, old, dank, and hot as hell, stagnation and despair are known ecologies that keep us from collective liberation.

I see this in movement formulas, where the vicious callout culture runs rampant. Eager to point the finger to avoid being labeled "unconscious" or worse. We develop analyses, hoping always to be on the "right side" of things. Then leaving little room for choice. For alternatives. The guilty must leave. Here there is no room for transformation.

What I dream of is not some magic kumbaya future where we are all healed. I dream of compassionate confrontation, of greater self- and collective care. So I try to reach for the compassion as often as I can stand and spread liberally all over the conditions.

I know that healing needs places to breathe radical hope, so I don't give up. When in doubt, I turn within to focus on my own vibration and trust that the resonance will bring in greater alignment, truth, and love.

Occupy

I am putting my body where words once stood. I am not alone.

There are a million ways folks settle into the ruins of the tropico-lonia.[3] They occupy everywhere. Here you will find squatted lands, borrowed buildings, work trades forged out of necessity, bravery, and hope. In each space members have worked out different levels of "per-missions" though each challenges the logic of private property. They embody other pathways through these actions. Some are agreements made between two who lack title, others—like the more than eighty thousand families who occupied abandoned parcels of land after arriv-ing to the city—fleeing the rural landscape in search of work, take up the lands of absentee landowners. Destroying a boundary, they occu-pied the coast and created homes with garbage and wood.

These are ancestors of today's politicized occupy movement. They are here in the abandoned buildings turned into social centers Casa Taft 169, El Hormiguero, la Casa Tomada and the closed schools turned into housing cooperatives and community spaces.

Although occupying has always been a technique of survival, after Hurricane Maria, occupying spread immensely. Almost all the cen-ters for mutual aid were established in abandoned buildings. Families create their own small-scale version of mutual aid too by moving into old schools after their homes were blown away, living with neighbors, extended family, and chosen kin.

Without access to intergenerational wealth, occupation is a strat-egy to reclaim place. I am eternally grateful for El Hormiguero, where I learned to see beauty in abandoned buildings half eaten by nature, time, and disregard. I see a powerful convergence between weeds, superpowers, and me. We find ways to thrive in the rubble. I am still growing roots like the trees unfazed by garbage piles and imposed lim-its, they implant belonging into buildings, through electricity plugs and everything man-made. In the land, persistence eventually triumphs over man-made illusions of control and dominance.

In the process of rematriating, I learn that home is first and foremost my body. My home is also anywhere I am supported and protected, by friends, chosen kin, and even acquaintances who have given me a place to live for trade or who have shared costs with me and kept spending down. Together we learn how to reclaim, remake, and rehabilitate.

To embody what one dreams is a kind of informed protest. As we embody I think we must keep on searching for ways to challenge the concept of ownership. I am visioning big even as I move toward simplicity. I am remembering and acting from a place of affirming our freedom, despite the conditions we may find ourselves in.

Every day I sing the liberation chant created by the Black Feminist Breathing Chorus:

> *My people are free.*

Every time I can remember, I move my life in rhythm with this affirmation.

> *My people are free.*

> *My people are free.*
> *Anjankatu*

Sovereignty and Coliberation in Times of Climate Justice

The weight of these climate changing times is heavy. Things are intensifying in ways I could not fully track in this book. Some of these impacts include widespread periods of drought and historic flooding, earthquake swarms that lasted for well over a year in the south from 2019–20, and the strongest hurricane to hit Puerto Rico in over a century. Mountain roads have continued to collapse in response to heavy rains. We've also faced long-lasting heat waves increasing in intensity and duration. Like others across the globe, we lived through the global pandemic of COVID-19. In Puerto Rico, this pandemic was accompanied by a particularly violent policing of stay-at-home orders, many of which kept us out of our forests and beaches, against scientific wisdom that being outdoors was one of the safest places to be, and a surge in relocated gringos liberated by relaxed work conditions of the moment. In the context of the near-broken healthcare system, many people were refused care at hospitals and told to stay at home if they were not feeling well.

Regionally, hurricanes have multiplied and intensified as well. In 2024, Hurricane Beryl was the first category 5 storm to develop in June in recorded in history. We cannot escape the consequences of a centuries-long disregard of the earth and our nonhuman kin. Our collective liberation requires we reckon with these shifts if we are to continue shaping a path toward justice.

How can we face this moment without losing ourselves and our sanity in the process? How do we move away from the practices of extraction and contamination when we face a palpable disregard for life every day in the form of widespread inequality, genocide, and war? Palestine is on my mind as I write these words. Many have remarked on the parallels between what was the process of setter colonialism in Turtle Island and this moment that are worth naming. To be watching genocide in real time gives life to the historical chronicles that offer us a similar image of cruelty born of the myth of supremacy. I think that Palestinians have showed the world the sheer necessity of fortifying ourselves with love when we approach those who hate us.[1] It's the act of affirming our worth and refusing disposability despite the rampant abuse that surrounds the everyday conditions of life within a genocide. Beyond the protests, and the boycotts, and the mutual aid, our job is to energetically refuse psychic numbing and hold watch, witness, and stay present. This in and of itself is a radical act in response to the relentlessness of the violence. We must always pay attention to avoiding falling into the same trap of superiority even as we affirm what we know to be true. It is not easy, but then neither is surviving a genocide.

The central challenge for me in reclaiming and embodying sovereignty lies in how to both acknowledge the changes taking place while also remembering that we are also always already impacting the world just by being alive. So I ask that we slow down to connect with the heart of the earth. I invite us to grieve and practice gentleness as if our life depended on it. From here, we may imagine pathways through. We might adapt, restore, and connect with the visions needed to open a new timeline if we're lucky. If not, we still may restore our spirits and intentionally contribute to the land's efforts to restore balance to this planet. In closing, dear reader, I provide a window into the smaller, more intimate actions and ancestral practices that have helped me endure in the face of the relentlessness of this moment.

It's hot. Again. We live without air conditioning. The heat pulses. There is a moment of coolness at sunrise. I try and get up and out to walk the dogs before 10:00 A.M. rolls in with warnings or advisories. Continual heat amidst high humidity feels like walking around in a cloud. It sticks to you and even breathing is a test of patience and consciousness.

The heat teaches me that it is impossible to continue to move in the same way I once did. I try to listen. Certainly, those of us organizing for collective liberation grapple with the urgency of the moment and constantly inhabit a contradictory space. We must respond to the conditions of the current reality and often work long hours, tracking, reacting, and resisting. This makes it challenging to truly allow ourselves to rest, or even slow down. Keeping busy is wise in many ways. In a system where our very survival and success depends on our productivity and our "competency," slowing down may spark buried feelings of inadequacy, shame, or even fear. It may have deep roots, ones that go even beyond our individual lives, into the generational pasts and traumas we may have inherited. And yet, "taking time" to rest and restore provides the clarity and the energy needed to interrupt and transform these patterns.

Tricia Hersey—Black American activist and performance artist and founder of the Nap Ministry—takes this a step further. When we rest, we can then mobilize from the worldview of our dreams. She acknowledges the difficulty when she notes that "truly practicing rest is a battle and liberation practice. No one wants you to deeply rest, because most people have never had the opportunity to practice it consistently, so there is no model for how to embody it."[2] Hersey calls on the descendants of enslaved Africans to accept their responsibility to dream in recognition of the privilege that their ancestors' survival makes possible in our lives today. Indeed, for those of us who have survived attempted genocide, slavery, and colonization, it is a gift and responsibility to dream. To dream is neither superficial or reactionary.

When I first heard the ritual song "Abrete corazon" (Open your heart), by Rosa Giove, it spoke to the shift I wish to move toward. As Giove offers in song, "Es tiempo ya / ya es ahora / ábrete el corazón / y recuerda / como el espíritu cura / como el amor sana / como el árbol florece / la vida perdura" (It is time / the time is now / open your heart / and remember / how spirit cures / how love heals / how the tree flowers / life endures).[3] These ritual lyrics remind me that the present moment is already here and that I am alive in it. Even in times of collapse, mass extinction, and grief, something else is being born. The next world, perhaps. And like all births, it cannot be rushed. It asks me always understand time from a longer point of view. From this perspective, it is possible to observe the continual cycles of life and death that are always operational and that we, as humans, do not control.

I grieve those mysterious cycles I do not understand or desire. I grieve the apparent decline of coqui frog's population in my own neighborhood. Even as we have tended the land and grown a small garden and urban forest within the context of a suburban style yard, filled densely with native plants, some chosen by us, others scattered by the wind, there are less of them than there were five years ago. When there was nothing but grass, a few palm trees, they sang loudly, interrupting evening phone calls and elevating the vibration of our home, anchoring us in the archipelago. But now, there are hot nights, and the sounds of air conditioning systems of my neighbors, an occasional cricket and the invasive Cuban toad frog. The coquí is also being displaced by climate change. I try to imagine that extinction is not guaranteed and keep my senses open to witness and learn from the earth. I celebrate the coquí when I hear them in other places. Coquí coquí. I hear you. I recognize you. Thank you for your life. I am grateful that I am not the wisest of the species, and let my grief empty into the earth, an offering to the medicine of regeneration inherent to the land. This grief is honorable. It reminds me that I am aware of and open to the web of life that I am a part of. My grief is a remembrance and a tribute. I am steadied by knowing it is relationships and the love they generate that heal us and allow us to live on.

When I attended the twenty-first Jornada Indígena Taína, I was reminded to be humble.[4] Imbalance has consequences, thus regaining and maintaining equilibrium is a perpetual practice. On this day in 2018, the elders told us that the earth would soon give birth to herself. We were advised to prepare by going into our hearts and connecting with love. The elders told us that the land knows how to heal. In other words, the earth doesn't depend on us to save her. Nature is always moving toward equilibrium in its own way. The antidote is always within reach. But if we wanted to survive alongside the land, we need to work on bringing equilibrium to our own actions and in our relations. We were advised to focus on healing our hearts and living from a place of deep integrity with all other life. Indeed, in climate justice a vision long fed by streams of indigenous wisdom, humans are not at the top of the pyramid but rather are the youngest, and most ignorant of all species. We must listen and be led into action based on understanding ourselves as one part of the whole, certainly not the most important of it.

When the earthquake swarms began in 2019, I could not get the image of the earth giving birth to herself out of my mind. More than nine thousand tremors later, I felt certain these were the contractions the elders spoke of. Itiba Cahubaba's next world emerging. If the story of the first birth of this cosmic navigator was filled with suffering and sacrifice, it is my hope that this next world will be different. Still, it is not always easy to decipher the messages the earth speaks. There must be a restoration of trust in our innermost voice, something that colonization has sought to decimate. It is the gentle breeze or light rain that comes as a blessing, or a just knowing at the base of one's being.

I find it helpful to look to the other beings who also inhabit the earth to discern the land's messages about collective liberation. We find another affirmation of the roots of our sovereign strength and resilience in trees, who are in native traditions thought of as the standing people. Their medicine is giving and rootedness.[5] For example, tabonuco (*Dacryodes excelsa*) is an ancient tree native to our archipelago (and the lesser Antilles as a whole) over five centuries old. It is slow growing and generally found in humid forests. It offers a beautiful white resin used by ancestors and present-day indigenous folx in ceremony to connect with the spirit realm. While searching for "scientific" research on the tabonuco, I found a guide by the USDA that offered an unethical harvest protocol by cutting open the tree that "spills out the resin when wounded." Instead, I have learned there is no need to wound the tree to receive the medicine since there is a time during the moon cycle when the tree will naturally release the resin. Gathering tabonuco resin when the letting go is initiated by the tree is the only time of an ethical harvest.

Tabonuco is one of the most resistant to hurricanes. The key to their strength is in its way of rooting. Tabonuco as a species of trees provide a network of support to one another underground via their root system that are linked to neighboring trees. This process creates a massive grounding within a community of tabonucos so powerful that even if they break at the top (they can grow up to 120 feet tall and the diameter of the trunk can grow up to 5 feet), it is unlikely that they will break from below. What might we learn from tabonuco in terms of our own actions toward sovereignty and coliberation?

Like the root system of a tabonuco forest, we are an ecosystem. Our roots are intertwined across space and time. Tabonuco remind us of the nurturing that is available to those who put down "roots." Rootedness helps us to maintain balance and stay healthy. Each one of our roots makes our neighbors stronger, provided we understand that our togetherness should never limit our individual growth. We can be reminded by the tabonuco to rely on one another and to live in gratitude for the blessings of our kin. We can remember that we are roots of the future, or as Veronica Agard puts it, ancestors in training.[6] The sovereignty that can be born from the wisdom of the land via the medicine of tabonuco is a spiritual sovereignty based on interdependence and autonomy.

Sovereignty is reciprocal. This reciprocity is sustained by our individual capacity to be rooted and embodied. One cannot feel sovereign if they have not cultivated a deep and inner sense of safety and trust in self. That ripples outward in relationships. But if we are not doing this work in community—being witnessed and witnessing, holding space, and being held, our individual practices will only go so far. This is the healing that comes from the realization that, as Ana Portnoy Brimmer argues, our freedom is native.[7] It is our birthright and already within us. Even amid collective amnesia, freedom continues to live on. When we live life as ceremony, we not only remember but also become that which we seek. The more we do this together, the more we learn to step fully into our sovereign power. When each of us is rooted in our own truth, it becomes possible for all of life to thrive.[8]

Since returning "home" to my ancestral lands, I have experienced deep transformations in my sense of sovereignty. After years of living far from my original homeland, rematriating helped me connect with waves of joy that derive from understanding and being connected to our inherent belonging to earth. It is an immense privilege from the perspective of spirit, even if it has meant more intensity and struggle in materials ways. The decision to rematriate was a balm to my spirit and feels like an embodied prayer in the face of wave after wave of intergenerational trauma and the ongoing displacement of Puerto Ricans from the archipelago. Nothing can take away the knowing that comes from connecting with the lands of my ancestors. Billions of years of wisdom lives in the earth, just below the surface. Returning to this land has awakened memories in me and restored my own sense of clarity and purpose. It has motivated me to reclaim my indigeneity, carefully and slowly by learning from elders and connecting to the ancestral plane—but consistently.

But physical rematration may not be possible, or ethical, for everyone. Under climate change we may decide to root where we are now, choosing to travel in airplanes less and less physically—whether by choice in response to how many resources airplanes consume. Either way, we will probably be forced by the earth (and political leaders) to "shelter in place" as many of us learned to do during the pandemic. Of course, travel is always possible in spiritual terms. We can all heal wherever we are by building a relationship with the land and seeing her for who she is: a sentient being who makes our life possible. As Frenak reminds us, "estamos en todos los lugares, porque en todo están nuestros ancestros, los ríos-montañas" (We are in all places because in everything are our ancestors, the river-mountains).[9] Everywhere we live on this earth, there is a way to access this fundamental connection with the land and to be changed by it. Rematriation may begin with a reclamation practice or a memory restored through genealogy studies, ritual, or ceremony. The important thing is to walk the ancestral path through ceremony, prayer, dreaming, patience, crafting, and listening.

Reclaiming requires a deeper field of observation and capacity to discern beyond the material.

When I began to connect more deeply to the land, I could see abundance everywhere. The earth gives more than we can consume; she lives in a constant cycle of love. Likewise, rematriation is always about return. Already a sea change has begun, and we are witnessing the expansion of a landback movement, among the most beautiful expressions of rematriation I have seen. For as we return the land to original stewards and heed the wisdom and the brilliance of indigenous elders, we are all liberated. To my mind, rematriation is the work of remembering that kinship is more than our blood lines—it is a practice of honoring indigenous wisdom and doing what one can to restore stewardship of the land to indigenous hands.

It has helped me to recall that, while I am living a material existence, everything is in a constant and unending cycle of change. The legend of El mago de Aguas Buenas (shaman of good waters) speaks to this sacred spiral. The medicine man prophecies a series of events just before his death in the late 1800s: hurricane, earthquake, revolution. I learn of this story much later in my journey and immediately recognize this pattern in present time.

What can we save at the end of a cycle? What can we steer? What can we release? The grief of death and loss is real, but it is also completely natural. Under the strictures of linear time that shape us collectively, maybe rebirth is the choice.

In the face of any challenge we can stay "dead" and allow what is no longer working to consume us or we can choose another path. Of course, our rebirth coexists with our aging so this release to begin again is not a "clean slate" (if such a thing ever did exist), but a messy, complex, and partial practice. Anyway, what is the actual beginning of our life? Did it begin with the start of this universe? The nebula that birthed us?

It is challenging to feel connected to abundance when there is so much inequality in the world. When extractive practices continue to intensify as they have in the Caribbean—be it through offshore deep-sea drilling, tourism, or mining—it feels challenging to see abundance reflected. But there it is, just out of view. We can see it when we trace the "products" extracted across borders and from bodies.

Just as our earth has been separated, we too have been separated. Coming together to support one another's liberation journeys is a radical act of healing. Coliberation requires solidarity in action. When engaging in cross-geographic acts of solidarity, it is essential to consider how to be led by people who have been directly impacted. Sometimes, I find the distinction between direct and indirect impacts harder to discern in our own communities. Still, there are important place-based differences that must be recognized as we work together for a free Boriké from our different positionalities across the globe.[10]

No coming home journey is the same but what they all have in common is the need to be humble, openhearted, and grateful. To listen before acting. To trust that when we are ready, the universe will give us what we need to take the next step. A large part of the journey is to unlearn and leave behind the unhealthy behaviors instilled in us by capitalism like greed, competition, and entitlement. That way we can be generous, responsible, and accountable community members. To share risk, we must each understand and use our privileges—be they based on our geographic location, our access to salaried work, or healthcare—to conspire to support others and open to being supported.

Each time I struggle to connect with possibility of a life beyond disaster, I remember the immediate aftermath of Hurricane Maria. The divisions between archipelago and diaspora dissolved in a way I had never witnessed before. As we weathered the storm, Lau and I listened to the radio reports before the signal dropped across the island, all the voices we heard were from folx based in the diaspora.

Some were already searching for updates on their family members and the towns where they resided, sending love via radio airwaves. After the storm, it was really our kin in the diaspora who organized and sent an immense number of resources to support those on the island.[11] As a people we faced such destruction, but we were also coming together. As in Rebecca Solnit's work on hope after disaster, my experience in the moments after the passage of the storm affirmed my deepest dreams.[12] There was radical possibility and surprisingly profound moments of solidarity and growth. We began to joke at home, "in nature, nothing is wasted." It became something like an affirmation: to escape the confines of the material world, we must tap into the knowledge of the earth—nothing is garbage. Everything can be reused, composted, or retrofitted. It's hard to continue in this practice as I am further distanced from the storm, but occasionally I remember. None of these comforts will be here forever. Nothing but change is promised. I believe deeply that these moments were a glimpse into the knowledge that not only was buried intentionally but also lives on, as Giove writes in her song, beneath the fire, beneath the water. Boriké has, since Hurricane

Maria, surprised me with the deep roots of solidarity in the form of mutual aid, rematriation, and badass organizing.

Still, it was hard to manage the expectations of "helping" activists, organizers, and nonprofits that held the best of intentions, but in practice reproduced certain inequalities between those on the ground and visitors. One example is folx came to visit with preexisting agendas or unsolicited advice about how to access funding streams rather than listening to what was needed. Others planned trips to the archipelago to volunteer, only reaching out after booking travel to ask that folxs on the ground do the vast majority of coordinating such trips for free. People who donated to funds later wanted to come see the impact of their money and expected site visits to be coordinated at their convenience.[13] The more coming from outside in terms of demands, the less energy on the ground to build from our own experience.

Look, travel if you want to. But before hopping on a plane, consider that the resources in the place you want to visit are already limited, especially after a climate event. I invite coliberators to imagine: How can I inject a space with more possibility before making a move? For example, during the pandemic, news spread about water rationing in Hawai'i for locals to make up for the excess being consumed by the sudden high incidence of tourist travel. Likewise, when water was being rationed in Puerto Rico due to lack of maintenance of our water reservoirs, the tourism industry went on with business as usual.

Diasporic Boricuas and allies alike could reclaim their sovereign power by moving resources associated with trips they do take with more intention. This could look like contracting a local small business or a person who does catering instead of going to a restaurant. While I appreciate the sentiment behind those who visited from the United States and invited big groups of organizers to eat lavish meals at expensive restaurants, these actions do very little to alter the material conditions on the ground. I think it's a great example of how we might move with more intention. Not only are we outsourcing our nourishment to big companies but we have zero control over the energetics behind the creation of the foods or the quality of the foods. Eating in a place that sources locally and hiring people instead of businesses is helpful. I wish for us to remember that feeding our people is ancestral medicine.

Another example to move resources with intention is buying a used car instead of spending on a monthlong car rental that could be then gifted to someone who doesn't already own one locally. Yes, this takes extra time, planning, and relationships on the ground to make possible. I know these are worth the effort.

Navigating layers of identity, privilege, and oppression requires a deep personal commitment to reflect on one's way of occupying space. In sharing my reflections about the ways we have been challenged, I do not intend to recreate a dynamic of "us versus them" or *"aqui* versus *alla"* (here versus there) but rather to see us in relationship to a problem. We must practice empathy even as we reckon with the inequalities we benefit from and in some cases reproduce in our everyday lives. To find ways to strengthen ourselves to resist and transform this reality, we must ask, how can we collectively source everything we need from each other?

The answers will not come quickly. Urgency is a learned speed imposed on us by the capitalist system. Urgency is a manifestation of the colonial logic of scarcity that keeps us from peace and joy. As we all know, the system has no interest in slowing down. Under late capitalism, it is precisely in those moments when people need to slow down, the system goes faster. Pushing through is easier when the population is tired and when we are in survival mode. It's up to us to settle into another logic, one that is older and wiser. It is up to us to let our actions be guided by the cyclical rhythm of the land.

What if we have more time than we think? I try to remember the time it takes for a volcano to shape an island or a glacier to form each time I feel myself fall back into the despair of urgent action, scarcity, or its shadow—apathy. The future is asking us to remember that no matter what has happened we are not tragic.[14] It is asking us to remember that these are times of prophecy, not pity. The future is asking us to remember that the place of our power is here and now in the eternal present.

When human impact has been so great, it can be easy to lose a sense of humility and recall that we are only a small part of a larger, wiser, ancient earth. To rebuild a sustainable ecosystem, we can begin anywhere, trusting that it will ripple out in time in ways we cannot imagine. As adrienne maree brown argued in a recent presentation for the Embodiment Institute, "the scale is depth and it is accessible."[15] I take this to mean big impact now occurs in our scale of influence—at the most intimate scale imaginable. We can harness the flow of inspiration and plant meaningful seeds of change into our cells and the soil. If the impacts of land, water, and energy use were where it all began, why not start with any of these? How might you enter into relationship with or deepen the relationship you have with your nonhuman kin? The elements? The land?

I have always found it helpful to nurture my dreams with the medicine of art. In the work of Boricua poet and activist Ana Portnoy Brimmer, I found a great support to arrest feelings of overwhelm and impotence. Her poem "Strawberries" disrupts the myth she was told as a child. Strawberries, like freedom, would never come to Puerto Rico because it didn't have the "climate." But high in the mountains, she eats wild strawberries while listening to a farmer who refuses multinational seeds to replace local coffee beans that were destroyed by Hurricane Maria. "We have to grow our own to be our own," the farmer in the poem remarks.[16] Portnoy Brimmer reminds me that collective liberation exists, it's as real as a wild strawberry. It can only be cultivated and harvested by us if we attend to what is in front of us, ignoring the myths we have been fed.

Life in the tropicolonia is full of surprises, contradictions, and joys. It helps me to remember that all poisons are cures in the right doses. Everything has the potential to be medicine if we integrate it. If we grieve and let go. There are certainly bleak currents, there is corruption, but there is also beauty. There is immense collective power here. Enough to oust a governor from power. Enough to stay.

Impossible things have occurred here in my time, and I am confident the future will continue to surprise me. I think it is helpful to remember that everything is vibration before it becomes matter. As a result, those of us invested in building anew from this destruction must take seriously the art of imagination and the importance of practice. What might our worlds and our communities feel like when we are free? We must channel and then anchor this uncensored vision of liberation.

I am here giving myself fully to the beauty, knowing that we will find our way through the conundrums of late capital and colonial unspeakability, and continue to make magic. It is my sincere wish that you, dear reader, will contribute to building liberation in this lifetime, for this is how we affirm our sovereignty. In each moment, in each decision, we can let go of fear, control, and worry. We can refuse victimhood. As we reclaim true abundance, let us loosen the collective unconscious contract that every act in the world can be measured along the lines of right and wrong. Let us abolish debt. Instead of living in a sense of indebtedness, let us build social relationships, freeing ourselves from disciplinary or punitive structures and shift to community-focused exchange based on mutual expectations, trust, and shared responsibilities. Amid systems collapse, climate change, and war, we can reach for healing found in community and creative imagination. We can adapt.

May we walk into the future remembering that life is ceremony.[17] May the sacred be restored in every act and in every breath. May we live to see this change take root.

Privileges and Responsibilities for Islanders and Diasporic Boricuas

We co-created this document for all CEPA collaborators to reflect on what it means to be in solidarity across geographic locations and positions at the start of this journey.[1] We believe Augusto Boal's definition of "sharing similar risk" is an important baseline for us as geographically dispersed peoples wanting to work together for the liberation of Borikén. In so many ways, we can see that solidarity has been vital to our existence as a project. It has kept CEPA alive but it has also led to frustrating and draining exchanges with our diaspora-based kin. We've come to understand that solidarity requires deep practice. For us, solidarity is a verb, requiring us to use our different levels of access and privilege to move toward coliberation.[2] This is our first effort to note the distinct rights and responsibilities for diaspora and island-based Boris. We believe that clarifying these differences will help us to promote healthy relationships between the multiple communities that make up Borikén. Our hope is that these words will help us to build bridges that allow us to be in reciprocal relationship cross-charco.[3]

Caution

We understand the identities that make up island and diasporic communities are not singular, but we still think there are important place-based differences that must be recognized and honored as we work together for a free Borikén from our different positionalities across the globe. To try and simplify, when we speak of islanders we are referring to those whose home base is Borikén and when we speak of diaspora we are

referring to those whose home base is somewhere outside the archipelago. If you have moved cross-charco in your lifetime, you may recognize
yourself in both these lists. Please read the following as a provocation
and a conversation starter.

Island Conditions

There are a multiplicity of realities within this archipelago. Overall, the
conditions of life on this archipelago get everyday more difficult and,
like many who live in the Caribbean, our lives are full of improvisation
and changes that we navigate in an attempt to survive. It's something
you can't appreciate entirely if you only come here to visit, no matter how long. Chances are, if you live in Puerto Rico you are being
grossly underpaid or have to create your own sources of income and be
extremely inventive to make ends meet. If you are one of the few that
is well paid, chances are high that you work for or receive funds from
an organization, business, or foundation that is based abroad. Some of
us also rely heavily on our diaspora connections for our own survival,
sending us food, money, or other resources.

The island's infrastructure is also extremely fragile. We regularly confront damaged homes, shortages of food, and water and power outages.
Fifteen minutes of heavy rain can lead to road closures and all kinds
of delays, including interruptions to phone or internet signal. Seeing
the doctor can take up to eight hours and getting an appointment can
take months. We have to take a number and wait. We pray to never fall
ill on the weekend. Although it is possible to access local organic food,
they are quite expensive, and eating out is difficult for any vegetarian or
vegan, or anyone looking to eat greens or food without pesticides. Even
commercial imported food one can access in the supermarkets is much
more expensive than in the United States and of lower quality, given the
distance it must travel.

Islanders also regularly witness outsiders (including English-speaking
white-passing Boris) receive better treatment and get the best of what
our island has to offer. We are witnessing firsthand the privatization and
displacement of our kin and loved ones, while we watch the influx of
white folx and diasporicans, who are deeply disconnected to island realities, come in and make a life for themselves. We do not feel the same
way about return diaspora and white entrepreneurs, but when diaspora
folx show up with ideas about how to "fix" things on the island based on

what they know, it can feel very exploitative at worst and pushy or naive at best. When diasporic Boris are coming just to visit, we are expected to travel long distances last minute to meet up with folx who just don't "have the time" to come to our part of town.

Islander Privileges

- Islanders are able to connect with the land and ocean; they often can access traditional foods and native medicinal plants through foraging.
- Islanders can see firsthand what is happening in Boriké and don't have to rely on fake news or personal connections to find out what is happening here.
- Islanders live in a tropical climate that changes ten degrees throughout the year and do not have to face hard winters.
- Islanders are living on their ancestral lands; this makes it easier to connect with a sense of inherent belonging.
- Islanders haven't had their authenticity challenged. In many ways they get to determine what it means to be Boricua.

Islander Responsibilities

- Islanders can document the work that is happening on the ground. They can attend protests and witness firsthand the realities of life in Borikén. They have a responsibility to share the truth of their experience with folx from the diaspora.
- With humidity, salt, and rapid climate change shaping our islands, islanders have to constantly navigate accelerated decay rate and have a responsibility to change their consumption patterns.
- When accessible, islanders seek out locally sourced foods, take up foraging, and reclaim forgotten plants and nutrients around them in the environment.
- Islanders respect and embrace the members of their community who live abroad. Rather than viewing the diaspora as a group of people who are "less Puerto Rican" or "assimilated," they have a responsibility to recognize the reality and pain of their displacement.

- We ask that islanders listen and learn from the diaspora about the intersectional nature of oppression and examine the realities of racism, classism, transphobia, and sexism present in the archipelago.
- Protecting, healing, and nurturing the land requires all of us to give back. This is an incredibly important responsibility to steward and sustain life on these islands.

Diaspora Conditions

A single diaspora experience does not exist, although studies have tended to focus on (and maybe overemphasize) the Boris who are *en vaiven* (in movement).[4] We know that there are a multiplicity of realities that compel people to out-migrate. Studies show that once you are in the diaspora for three generations, there tends to be much less movement, although the archipelago is still a crucial part of folx's identity formation, whether they have stepped foot on the island or not. For the purposes of our thinking, we'd like to highlight three specific forms of inhabiting diaspora: displaced, nomadic, and rematriator in process. If you have been displaced by Hurricane Maria or due to other recent climate events or economic factors, we recognize you may not be able to travel often. If your family was displaced earlier in history, you may no longer have direct connections to the island, making travel unlikely. If you are nomadic, you may routinely visit the island but may not have a full-time job, contributing to a level of economic insecurity that keeps you from putting down roots in Borikén. If you are a rematriator in process, you may be visioning a countercurrent move to Borikén to build the resistance yet still unsure how to make that transition.

Regardless of which of these identities best fits yours, diasporicans may experience a sense of uprootedness and otherness. Diasporicans (also Diasporic Boricuas) can feel homesick for Boriké and then come here and feel totally disregarded, less valuable, or unaccepted, especially if they do not speak Spanish well. Early efforts to reconnect often bring up more wounding as islanders frequently scold diasporic Boris for "losing" their way, or want to correct our Spanish, or other subtle practices aimed at invalidating and dismissing those who did not stay. The newest version of this "yo no me quito" disregards that many of us were forced to leave and do not have the economic security, health, or other privileges to return. No one seems to recognize that these were realities that we did not choose. Although many diasporicans have spent their lives resisting colonization and speaking out against the inequalities in Puerto Rico, they are rarely acknowledged for those efforts. Many diasporicans feel that they are treated as an extension of the colonizer. Although many were shocked by Donald Trump's treatment of Puerto Rico after Hurricane Maria, diasporicans were not. It isn't a surprise for most diasporic folx that the United States isn't and won't be supportive of Puerto Rico's liberation, just as it hasn't been supportive of Black and Brown communities.

Diaspora Privileges

- Diasporic Boris do not have to engage with the transformations of the island's daily as a result of disaster capitalism, rising religious fundamentalism, and gender violence. This allows them to maintain a degree of nostalgia for life at home without directly navigating the current conditions of life at home.
- Diasporicans often practice their culture as a form of resistance. Therefore they often dismiss islanders as being "colonized" or less "woke," not realizing that Puerto Rican culture is always in a constant process of evolution.
- Diasporicans can decide how much they would like to engage with inefficiencies and difficulties that are an unavoidable part of daily life in the archipelago.
- Diaspora-based Boris often have access to better housing and a greater area of movement than islanders do that may allow them some distance from restrictions in their freedom of speech or living in communities where fundamentalism and physical violence are constantly a threat.
- On the whole, diasporicans have more access to resources, jobs, and better pay, and often can secure full-time employment with salary and benefits appropriate to their level of experience and training. While their life is a hustle, they rarely have to live with the same level of precarity that is commonplace on the island.
- Diasporic Boris often live in diverse cities and can make connections with other diasporic communities. This helps them to understand themselves in relationship to other oppressed groups globally.

Diaspora Responsibilities

- Boris abroad are in a position to affect US policies and attitudes that will directly shape conditions of life on the island. They have a responsibility to leverage the special advantages, rights, and benefits to which they have access to shape US and international political opinion on Puerto Rican issues.
- Diaspora Boris who are actively practicing solidarity could share stories about what is happening in the archipelago. They have a responsibility to use their access to help islanders obtain a platform to share their experiences directly with interested allies and coliberators.
- We invite diaspora folx to move resources intentionally so that they contribute to long-term sustainability of projects and people living in the archipelago. This includes but is not limited to applying for grants, sending no-strings attached monetary and in-kind donations, investing in solar and regenerative methods of energy production, and participating in the creation of interdependence and noncapitalist exchanges. When in doubt, ask!

References/Shout Out

We are thankful to the work of diaspora thinkers Romesh Hettiarachi and Yasmin Hernandez who have offered amazing pieces of writing that tease out the differences between home and diaspora communities. Their works, "Diaspora Responsibilities: The (Mis)Conception of Diaspora Privilege" and "Repatriation: Critical Concept Missing in Relief Efforts," respectively, served as model and inspiration for this writing.[5]

NOTES

Introduction

1. I will use "Puerto Rico" and "Boriké," the indigenous name of the island archipelago, interchangeably in this text. It is most often spelled Boriken, but also less often as Boriké or Boh'li'kin. Any of these names are more accurate than the colonized name of Puerto Rico. My personal preference to use Boriké is a result of my commitment to decolonization, a practice that can begin with our language choices.

2. "Mixed race" is a loaded concept everywhere, especially in the Latin American context, where the myth of racial democracy is particularly insidious. Rather than there being harmony and equality between the three "races" of our origin (indigenous, black, and European) the idea of mixing always contained a promise of whitening, or improving one's origins, revealing violent subtexts around desired erasure of blackness and indigeneity. Although both my parents identify as Puerto Ricans and share a very similar class background—they grew up in the South Bronx in the same public housing complex—each occupies a different location racially. My mom is white, and my dad is black. My mother's mixed-ness is the product of a New York romance as my maternal grandfather was Puerto Rican, and my grandmother was a first-generation Italian American. But that's a story for another time. I still use the term "mixed race" because it marks my childhood experiences, which could vary widely depending on the parent I was with. I grew up very aware of my racial ambiguity. Within a US racial system and hierarchy, mixed race feels like it indexed my experience living as a diasporic Boricua. Despite the privileges, erasures, and ambiguities that can be commonplace in a world organized around white supremacy, my commitment is to reclaiming and remembering the afro-indigenous technologies, worldviews, and practices of my ancestry.

3. Prentis Hemphill's work as therapist, writer and founder of the Embodiment Institute has inspired me in this walk. See their recent work: *What It Takes to Heal: How Transforming Ourselves Can Change the World* (New York: Random House, 2024).

4. Gina Ulysse, *Why Haiti Needs New Narratives: A Post-Quake Chronicle* (Middletown, CT: Wesleyan University Press, 2015).

5. During this time I was able to confirm that I had severe endometriosis, a condition inherited from my mother. I have been doing a lot of thinking about the relationship between chronic conditions and historical trauma, especially how the legacy of patriarchy impacts our ability to creatively birth new worlds. There are weavings between this condition and my turn toward rematriation that are not actively traced in this writing but will be a part of future work I am now developing for a collection of works on Puerto Rican feminisms edited by Jessica Pabón forthcoming with Feminist Press.

6. It all began, some say, with Tarek El-Tayeb Mohammed Bouazizi, a twenty-six-year-old Tunisian street vendor who set himself on fire on December 17, 2010, becoming a catalyst for movements in Tunisia, later in Egypt and across the Arab world where many stood up against autocratic regimes ready to give up their own life for equality and democratic participation.

7. See, e.g., Alberto Jimenez Corsín and Adolfo Estalella, "The Atmospheric Person: Value, Experiment, and Making Neighbors in Madrid's Popular Assemblies," *HAU: Journal of Ethnographic Theory* 3, no. 2 (2013): 119–39; Clare Solomon and Tania Palmieri, eds., *Springtime: The New Student Rebellions* (Brooklyn, NY: Verso Press, 2011); Jeffrey Juris and Maple Rasza, "Occupy, Anthropology, and the 2011 Global Uprisings," Hot Spots, *Fieldsights*, July 27, 2012, https://culanth.org/fieldsights/series/occupy-anthropology-and-the-2011-global-uprisings; and Manissa Maharawal, "Occupy Wall Street and a Racial Politics of Inclusion," *Sociological Quarterly* 54, no. 2 (2013): 177–81.

8 Fred Moten, *In the Break: The Aesthetics of the Black Radical Tradition* (Minneapolis: Minnesota University Press, 2003).

9. By using the term "tight spaces," I am referencing Danielle Goldman's *I Want to Be Ready: Improvised Dance as a Practice of Freedom* (Ann Arbor: University of Michigan Press, 2010), which offers a history of improvisation in dance. Her work is heavily influenced by Moten's *In the Break*. Building on this work, she argues that improvisation in and of itself is not equivalent to freedom. Rather, the dance between improvisation and form and the tight spaces betwixt and between the two practices allow for the realization of freedom.

10. Goldman, *I Want to Be Ready*, 22.

11. adrienne maree brown, *Emergent Strategy: Shaping Change, Changing Worlds* (Chico, CA: AK Press, 2017), contains a chart mapping the core elements of emergent strategy (50). They include fractal, adaptive,

interdependence and decentralization, nonlinear and iterative, resilience and transformative justice, and creating more possibilities.

12. Although Félix Guattari and Gilles Deleuze were writing much earlier, their philosophical project (1972–80) also drew on examples from the natural world to explore possibilities for resisting that exceeded the limits of capitalism. See, e.g., Félix Guattari and Gilles Deleuze, *Capitalism and Schizophrenia*, trans. R. Hurley, M. Seem, and H. R. Lane (New York: Viking Press, 1977). The "rhizome" (also known as rootstocks) is another natural phenomenon that has been generative for organizing efforts against global capitalism—a totalizing force the world over. A rhizome, containing multiple nodes from which roots and shoots originate, speaks to the power of decentralized organizing. Rhizomes grow perpendicular, permitting new shoots to grow out of the ground. This horizontal stem forms new roots and shoots, and each can live on after it is cut from the parent plant. Guattari and Deleuze, channeling the rhizome, reminded us that no future can be entirely limited by the past and that we could continually grow into new organisms, ceaselessly connected through circumstance and multiplicity.

13. Kevin Quashie, *Black Aliveness, or a Poetics of Being* (Durham, NC: Duke University Press, 2021)

14. Deborah B. Gould, *Moving Politics: Emotion and ACT UP's Fight Against AIDS* (Chicago: University of Chicago Press, 2009).

15. LittleSis is a grassroots watchdog network and power-mapping organization. The works they published by Abner Dennis are extremely helpful for understanding the key players in the debt crisis: see, e.g., "COVID-19 and the Collapse of Private Hospitals in Puerto Rico." *LittleSis*, April 9, 2020, https://news.littlesis.org/2020/04/09/covid-19-and-the-collapse-of-private-hospitals-in-puerto-rico/, as well as his other articles at https://news.littlesis.org/author/abner-dennis/. Hedge Clippers have written several white papers on the impact of hedge funds and private equity firms on US economies: http://hedgeclippers.org/hedgepapers/topic/puerto-rico/. Lastly, Committee for Better Banks is a US nationwide campaign led by former and current bank workers who collaborated with Hedge Clippers on the revolving-door study of key actors in Puerto Rico's debt crisis.

16. See, e.g., Aloysha Goldstein, "Promises Are Over: Puerto Rico and the Ends of Decolonization," *Theory & Event* 19, no. 4 (2016): 1–14; Naomi Klein, *The Battle for Paradise: Puerto Rico Takes on the Disaster Capitalists*, trans. Teresa Córdova Rodríguez (Chicago: Haymarket Books, 2018); Stephen Park and Tim R. Samples, "Puerto Rico's Debt Dilemma and Pathways toward Sovereign Solvency," *American Business Law Journal* 54, no. 9 (2017), https://ssrn.com/abstract=2826301; and Rocío Zambrana,

Colonial Debts: The Case of Puerto Rico (Durham, NC: Duke University Press, 2021). For an investigative journalist perspective, see Ed Morales, *Fantasy Island: Colonialism, Exploitation, and the Betrayal of Puerto Rico* (New York: Bold Type Books, 2019). The website Puerto Rico syllabus (www.puertoricosyllabus.com) is a great source for collected news articles and other open-access pieces that explain various elements of the debt crisis. Also excellent is the Centro de Periodismo Investigativo (Center for Investigative Journalism; http://periodismoinvestigativo.com), which has tracked a range of issues related to the debt crisis and mismanagement of relief funds post-Maria, as well as led high-profile legal cases to challenge the lack of public access to documents related to both.

17. Diane Lourdes Dick, "U.S. Tax Imperialism in Puerto Rico," *American University Law Review* 65, no. 1 (2015): 1–87, offers an extensive review of economic imperialism the United States committed in the case of Puerto Rico. See also H. Whiteside, "Foreign in a Domestic Sense: Puerto Rico's Debt Crisis and Paradoxes in Critical Urban Studies," *Urban Studies* 56, no. 1 (2019): 147–66, https://doi.org/10.1177/0042098018768483.

18. Ayuda Legal is a nonprofit offering legal advocacy, education and general support to poor communities in Puerto Rico. They support an array of topics like mortgages, title, public housing, evictions, disaster, gender violence, voters rights and more. Learn more at https://ayudalegalpr.org.

19. Zambrana, *Colonial Debts*, 40.

20. Zambrana, *Colonial Debts*, 14.

21. Zambrana, *Colonial Debts*, 45.

22. Ariadna Godreau-Aubert, *Las propias: Apuntes para una pedagogía de las endeudadas* (San Juan, PR: Ediciones Emergentes, 2017), 15.

23. Laurent Dubois, *Haiti: The Aftershocks of History* (London: Picador Press, 2012), or for a documentary look at the financial controls imposed by debt adjustment in Jamaica, see Stephanie Black, dir., *Life and Debt* (2001). On the IMF, see Jake Johnston and Juan Antonio Montecino, "Jamaica: Macroeconomic Policy, Debt and the IMF," May 2011, https://www.cepr.net/documents/publications/jamaica-qr-2011-04.pdf; and Kevin Edmonds, "A Stellar Record of Failure: the IMF and Jamaica," The Other Side of Paradise (NACLA blog), May 11, 2012 https://nacla.org/blog/2012/5/11/stellar-record-failure-imf-and-jamaica.

24. Yarimar Bonilla and Marisol Lebrón, *Aftershocks of Disaster: Puerto Rico Before and After the Storm* (New York: Haymarket Press, 2019).

25. Klein *La batalla por el paraíso* (The battle for paradise), 49–60. Klein's visit to Puerto Rico ended in this publication, which builds upon and expands her understanding of the "shock doctrine" as she first authored

it in her 2007 publication *The Shock Doctrine: The Rise of Disaster Capitalism.* The book traces the origins of disaster capitalism to the University of Chicago under Milton Friedman with global impacts. In essence, "the shock doctrine" is a practice of using the public's disorientation following moments of massive trauma be they manmade political disasters or natural disasters to achieve control on the population and imposing "free-market" reforms.

26. Bonilla and LeBrón, *Aftershocks,* 9.

27. Raquela Salas Rivera, "no se cambia una chaqueta por una chaqueta," in *lo terciario / the tertiary* (Blacksbury, VA: Noemi Press, 2019), 24–27.

28. Ailton Frenak, *Ancestral Future,* ed. Rita Carelli, trans. Alex Brostoff and Jamille Pinheiro Dias (Cambridge: Polity Press), 36.

29. Marisol LeBrón, *Against Muerto Rico: Lessons from the Verano Boricua* (Cabo Rojo, PR: Editora Educación Emergente, 2021).

30. Yarimar Bonilla, "The Swarm of Disaster," *Political Geography* 78 (2020), https://doi.org/10.1016/j.polgeo.2020.102182.

31. Cecilia Aldarondo, dir., *Landfall,* Blackscrackle Films, 2020.

32. Mimi Sheller, *Island Futures: Caribbean Survival in the Anthropocene* (Durham, NC: Duke University Press, 2020).

33. Garriga-López, *Debt and Resurgence,* 124.

34. Garriga-López, *Debt and Resurgence,* 124, 126

35. David Graeber, *Debt: The First 5,000 Years* (London: Melville House, 2011).

36. Harney and Moten, *Undercommons,* 153.

37. Special thank you to Taraneh Farazeli and Toi Scott for showing me how to practice disability justice. Over the years that I have lived in Puerto Rico, I have come to recognize myself as a person with chronic illness and I have learned a lot about slowing down by learning from my comrades who have for a long time understood ability in ways I am only beginning to accept.

38. Dr. Eve Tuck is an Alaska Native (Unangax), who not only is an important theorist of rematriation but also committed to the practice of it. Her work is largely available online for download. She is one of the conveners along with K. Wayne of the Land Relationships Super Collective whose mission is to decolonize and heal relationships to land. The group works with five community organizations including the Black Land Project, Métis in Space, Ogimaa Mikana, Underground Center, and Sogorea Te' Land Trust. See http://www.landrelationships.com.

39. For more information on Yasmin's vision of rematriation, please visit her website https://rematriatingboriken.com.

40. Tony Castanha, *The Myth of Indigenous Caribbean Extinction* (New York: Palgrave Macmillan, 2010).

41. This popular understanding was later challenged by several scholars who researched maternal ancestries that showed a more complex picture. See Juan C. Martínez-Cruzado et al., "Reconstructing the Population History of Puerto Rico by Means of mtDNA Phylogeographic Analysis," *American Journal of Physical Anthropology* 128, no. 1 (2005): 131–55, https://doi.org/10.1002/ajpa.20108.

42. Pablo Navarro-Rivera, "Acculturation under Duress: The Puerto Rican Experience at the Carlisle Indian Industrial School 1898–1918," *Centro Journal* 18, no. 1 (2006): 222–59.

43. For example, see Margarita Nogueras-Vidal's academia.edu website for any number of works' including a 2011 publication, "Taino Symbolisms of Boriké," https://www.academia.edu/33913952/taino_symbolism_english_booklet_for_pdf_pdf, or Alfonso Peralta's forthcoming book *Karibe Ancestral: Manual de Cultural Ancestral y Pueblos Originarias del Caribe*. Pluma Barbara, organizer and indigenous activist based out of the Center for Mutual Aid in Lares (CAM JI) and founder of La Escuela Indígena de Formación y Saberes Ancestrales de Boriké and countless others who share wisdom in the old way—through oral history and practice—thank you.

44. For another argument in favor of indigenous resurgence in Puerto Rico, see Fáanofo Lisaclaire Uperesa and Adriana Garriga-Lopez, "Contested Sovereignties: Puerto Rico and America Samoa," in *Sovereign Acts: Contesting Colonialism Across Indigenous Nations and Latinx America*, ed. Frances Negron-Muntaner (Tucson: University of Arizona Press), 39–81.

45. Cara Page and Erica Woodland, *Healing Justice Lineages: Dreaming at the Crossroads of Liberation, Collective Care and Safety* (Berkeley, CA: North Atlantic Books, 2023).

46. The definitive text on the origins of healing justice is Cara Page and Erica Woodland, *Healing Justice Lineages: Dreaming at the Crossroads of Liberation, Collective Care and Safety* (Berkeley, CA: North Atlantic Books, 2023). Leah Lakshmi Piepzna-Samarasinha's "Not-so-brief personal history of the healing justice movement" is also a good primer for people just starting out: https://micemagazine.ca/issue-two/not-so-brief-personal-history-healing-justice-movement-2010–2016. Also worth naming are the people who have led or are leading this work, including Kindred Collective, Healing by choice!, Harriet's Apothecary, Fireweed Collective, and the National Queer and Trans Therapists of Color Network.

47. Gloria Anzaldúa, *Borderlands/La Frontera: The New Mestiza* (San Francisco: Aunt Lute Press, 1987); Susan Griffin, *A Chorus of Stones: The*

Private Life of War (New York: Anchor Books, 1992); bell hooks, *Ain't I a Woman? Black Women and Feminism* (Boston: South End Press, 1981); Audre Lorde, *Sister Outsider: Essays and Speeches* (Berkeley, CA: Crossing Press, 1984); Trinh Minh-Ha, *Woman, Native, Other: Writing Postcoloniality and Feminism* (Indianapolis: Indiana University Press, 1989); Toni Cade Bambara, ed., *The Black Woman: An Anthology* (New York: New American Library, 1970).

48. Mark Schuller, *Humanity's Last Stand: Confronting Global Catastrophe* (New Brunswick, NJ: Rutgers University, 2021); Ulysse, *Why Haiti Needs New Narratives*.

49. Catherine Walsh, "Decolonial Praxis: Sowing Existence-Life in Times of Dehumanities," keynote presentation, IX Congress of the International Academy of Practical Theology, Sao Leopoldo, Brazil, April 5, 2019, https://iapt-cs.org/ojs/index.php/iaptcs/article/view/189/624.

50. Macarena Gómez-Barris, *The Extractive Zone: Social Ecologies and Decolonial Perspectives* (Durham, NC: Duke University Press 2017).

51. Gómez-Barris, *Extractive Zone*, 10.

52. Nelson Maldonado-Torres, "Outline of Ten Theses on Coloniality and Decoloniality," 7, http://caribbeanstudiesassociation.org/docs/Maldonado -Torres_Outline_Ten_Theses-10.23.16.pdf.

53. Eve Tuck and K. Wayne Yang, "Decolonization Is Not a Metaphor," *Decolonization: Indigeneity, Education & Society* 1, no. 1 (2012): 1–40.

54. Melissa Rosario, "Intimate Publics: Autoethnographic Meditations on the Micropolitics of Resistance," *Anthropology and Humanism* 39, no. 1 (2014): 36–54.

55. Cherrie Moraga, "An Irrevocable Promise: Staging the Story Xicana," in *Radical Acts: Theatre and Feminist Pedagogies of Change*, ed. Ann Elizabeth Armstrong and Kathleen Juhl (San Francisco: Aunt Lute Books, 2007): 34–46.

Chapter 1

1. Rosa Clemente also tracked the dark side of "relief" work in her docuseries *PR on the Map*, https://pronthemap.com, from 2017–18. For a personal account of one Puerto Rican's experience with the vast distinction between visitors to the island and the realities that folks were living post-Maria, see Aurora Santiago Ortiz, "Testimonia as Stitch Work: Undoing Coloniality Through Autoethnography in Puerto Rico," *Chicana/Latina Studies: The Journal of Mujeres Activas en Letras y Cambio Social* 20, no. 2 (2021): 122–48. Santiago Ortiz describes these ironies based on her visit

to the island as a graduate student eating in restaurants powered by generators and intermingling with her own memories of earlier hurricanes while she lived on the island as a child.

2. Thank you to Nicolle Managelli of Radical Emprints for this gorgeous phrase.

3. The research team that helped identify the number of deaths post-Maria randomly selected 3,299 households in Puerto Rico to survey over the course of three weeks in January 2018. People in those homes reported a total of thirty-eight deaths. The scientists then extrapolated that finding to the island's total population of 3.4 million people to estimate the number of deaths. The researchers subtracted deaths recorded during that same period in 2016 and concluded that the mortality rate in Puerto Rico had jumped 62 percent in the three months following the storm. Given the small sample, it is very possible that the estimated death toll of 4,645 is still low. See Nishant Kishora, Domingo Marqués, Ayesha Mahmud, Mathew V. Kiang, Imary Rodriguez, Arlan Fuller, Peggy Ebner, Cecilia Sorensen, Fabio Racy, Jay Lemery, Leslie Mass, Jennifer Leaning, et al., "Mortality in Puerto Rico after Hurricane Maria," *New England Journal of Medicine* 379 (2018): 162–70, https://doi.org/10.1056/NEJMsa1803972.

4. For more information on the warehouse scandal, see "Gobierno pide mantener en sobre sellado y guardado en una bóveda el informe sobre el almacén de suministros," Centro de Periodismo Investigativo, March 5, 2020, https://periodismoinvestigativo.com/2020/03/en-sobre-sellado-y-guardado-en-una-boveda-del-tribunal-el-informe-sobre-el-almacen-de-suministros-en-ponce/; Carla Minet, "Papelón tras papelón en el caso del almacén de Ponce," Centro de Periodismo Investigativo, March 8, 2020, https://periodismoinvestigativo.com/2020/03/papelon-tras-papelon-en-el-caso-del-almacen-de-ponce/; or "Gobierno entrega a la prensa informe de almacén de suministros," Centro de Periodismo Investigativo, March 13, 2020, https://periodismoinvestigativo.com/2020/03/gobierno-entrega-a-la-prensa-informe-de-almacen-de-suministros/.

Chapter 2

1. Similar protests have been organized at the public art school Escuela de Artes Plásticas, located in Old San Juan. For more on the use of art in protests, see Katherine Everhart "Cultura-Identidad: The Use of Art in the University of Puerto Rico Student Movement, 2010," *Humanity & Society* 36, no. 3 (2012): 198–219; or Melissa Rosario, "Public Pedagogy in the Creative Strike: Destabilizing Boundaries and Reimagining Resistance

in the University of Puerto Rico," *Curriculum Inquiry* 45, no. 1 (2015): 52–68

2. An in-depth focus of the history of protests at the UPR is beyond the scope of this book. Beginning as early as 1919, students were organizing against US intervention. I highly recommend Luis Nieves Falcón and Ineke Cunningham y Israel Rivera, *Huelga y Sociedad: Analisis de los sucesos en la U.P.R. 1981–1982* (Río Piedras, PR: Editorial Edil, 1982), for a close look at a powerful period of protests at the institution.

3. As filmmaker and journalist Juan C. Dávila Santiago argues, the working class is shrinking and an emerging class, the precariat, is growing. Dávila follows this precariat class in a documentary, *La generacion del estanbi* (*The Stand-by Generation*) (New York: Third World Newsreel, 2015), which he directed and produced. It explores the lives of a diverse group of young college graduates in Puerto Rico who are filling temporary jobs with low pay that constantly threaten their financial stability and future. Many in the film describe their lives as "on hold." They can't move out of their parents' house and often delay marriage and creating their own family because they simply don't have the income to be financially independent. The first time I watched it, I was surprised to see faces from my years studying the student mobilizations of 2010 and 2011. Although shocking, it further strengthened my conviction that what students are fighting for in the university is a transformation of the conditions of their near future, of their life as adults.

4. For those unfamiliar, the PPD is considered a more liberal party from within the context of the two-party system. They are the party who favors the status quo of the commonwealth in referendum held to contemplate the political future of the archipelago. The PNP or the statehood party is considered more conservative and pro-American. Though I don't think there's a one-to-one association between the US party system and the local one, but in general PPD would be considered more democratic PNP is more Republican. Giovanni Roberto's remarks come from a self-published piece he wrote for CDPEC before Hurricane Maria. Cáez, "Huelga 2017 en la mirada del CUCA 2005," Centro para el Desarrollo Político, Educativo y Cultural, April 20, 2019, https://www.cdpecpr.org/single-post/huelga -2017-en-la-mirada-del-cuca-2005.

5. For a diverse analysis of the dialogue generated as a result of this mobilization, see "Public Education: Crisis and Dialogue at the University of Puerto Rico," ed. Maritza Stanchich, special issue, *Sargasso* no. 1 (2011–12), https://dloc.com/UF00096005/00038/2j.

6. A public-private alliance is a long-term arrangement between government and private sector. The private entities usually provide initial

financing in exchange for profit generated over the life of the contract. These alliances usually set the stage for privatization of public resources over time.

7. Their charges included the classic list of "trumped up" charges: use of violence or intimidation against public authority, aggravated harm, aggravated restriction of freedom and for violating the right of assembly. In addition, four students were charged with inciting a riot.

8. I offer a microhistory of Comedores Sociales on page 69.

9. Verónica Figueroa Huertas, "Intervención femenina en la huelga 2017: Más allá de rostros y números," *Diálogo*, April 1, 2018, https://dialogo.upr.edu/intervencion-femenina-en-la-huelga-2017-mas-alla-de-rostros-y-numeros/.

10. John Holloway, *Change the World without Taking Power: The Meaning of Revolution Today* (London: Pluto Press, 2003).

11. See Melissa Rosario, "Ephemeral Spaces, Undying Dreams: Social Justice Struggles in Contemporary Puerto Rico" (PhD diss., Cornell University, 2013), 53–80.

Chapter 3

1. In a 2020 study of four independent data sets, the authors estimate that anywhere from four to seventeen percent of the population left Puerto Rico in one year's time (July 2017–18). Rolando Acosta et al., "Quantifying the Dynamics of Migration after Hurricane Maria in Puerto Rico," *PNAS* 117, 51 (): 2772–32778, https://doi.org/10.1073/pnas.2001671117.

2. Frances Negron-Muntaner, "The Emptying Island: Puerto Rican Expulsion in Post-Maria Time," *Emisferica* 14, no. 1 (2018), https://hemisphericinstitute.org/en/emisferica-14–1-expulsion/14–1-essays/the-emptying-isl and-puerto-rican-expulsion-in-post-maria-time.html.

3. Cloé Georas, "Native of Nowhere," in *Puerto Rican Jam: Rethinking Colonialism and Nationalism*, ed. Frances Negrón-Muntaner and Ramon Grosfoguel (Minneapolis: University of Minnesota Press, 1997), iv–xi.

4. The beaches belong to the people under article 6, section 19, of Puerto Rico's constitution and according to which the government must conserve, develop, and use its natural resources for the general welfare of the community.

5. There is a myriad of negative impacts to tourism in the Caribbean, from natural habitat loss, reduction in biodiversity, strain on resources, to pollution, and more. For a reference that explores how creatives mitigate

and resist such damage, see Angelique V. Nixon, *Resisting Paradise: Tourism, Diaspora and Sexuality in Caribbean Culture* (Jackson: University Press of Mississippi, 2015)

6. Zaire Zenit Dinzey-Flores, *Locked In, Locked Out: Gated Communities in a Puerto Rican City* (Philadelphia: University of Pennsylvania 2013).

7. For those unfamiliar, Isla Verde is a popular tourist destination located just across the road from San Juan's international airport. Only a few entrances to the beach remain public. The rest can be accessed only through hotels or high-rise apartment complexes that line the strip.

8. Key organizers of this press conference were attorney Jessica Rodríguez Martinez, Director Wanda Colón of the Caribbean Project for Justice and Peace, and Director Ariel Lugo of the USDA's International Institute for Tropical Forestry.

9. In practice, the ZMT is difficult to delimit because it is changeable. It is composed of the land covered by high tide. Ideally, all development should happen outside the ZMT to prevent unnecessary erosion and destruction of construction projects in the medium and long-term.

10. In the post-Maria context, this trend continues. On December 28, 2016, the historic Institute of Cultura Puertorriqueña based in Old San Juan was under contract by the land administration of the commonwealth to be developed into a fifty-three-room hotel. See the contract at https://drive.google.com/file/d/1aZhkVBZydsPHm981F2t4HFCOpp_Hllj3/view.

11. CFR's original mission was to build and maintain a diverse number of recreational facilities across the island, including all the public bathing areas (*balneario*). The development of the island's recreation facilities was subsidized by a special tax on hotel occupants, cementing an awkward relationship between tourism and public access to the shore. Although its main function was to manage public bathing areas, CFR was also empowered to build "recreational" facilities, which was interpreted broadly to support tourist initiatives and consumption of the island's natural resources.

12. Amigos del M.A.R. was founded in 1995, known for its efforts to defend the island's natural resources through education, consciousness raising, and direct actions denouncing criminal destruction of the island archipelago. It has become a formal nonprofit organization today focusing on citizen action to prevent the privatization of the coastline. To participate in their costal mapping of threats to coastal access visit www.mapadecostaspr.com.

13. María Benedetti, *Árboles nuestros para la supervivencia* (Bogotá, Colombia: Nomos "Ceiba," 2020), 97–105.

14. To read more about these challenges, see Rosario, "Intimate Publics."

15. Antonio Fernós, *De San Jerónimo a Paseo Caribe* (San Juan, PR: Ediciones Puerto, 2008). This book traces the origins of the Paseo Caribe case and offers an analysis of chain of ownership beginning with the transfer of title to Lieutenant Commander Virgil Baker of the US Navy who acquired the lands in 1926. Fernós was an active participant in the people's court led by several lawyers and professors in 2007 designed to oppose the construction plans and catalyze public outcry against it.

16. Paseo Caribe also included a small hotel for sale for $1.5 million that didn't sell until after Hurricane Maria. It is now called Costa Bahia and the owner is Eduardo Artau Gomez who made his fortune working in the healthcare system. The entire Metro Pavia Health System is controlled by the Artau family, who also own a staggering number of public hospitals as well as the insurance company First Medical. For a detailed history of the family in relationship to the collapse of private hospitals on the island, see Abner Dennis, "COVID-19 and the Collapse of Private Hospitals in Puerto Rico," LittleSis, April 9, 2020, https://news.littlesis.org/2020/04/09/covid-19-and-the-collapse-of-private-hospitals-in-puerto-rico/.

17. Governmental debates about this parcel of land began in 2003 when the House of Representatives approved a resolution to investigate whether the earlier construction projects on the islet of San Juan violated the Land Use Plan, especially after reports given about the construction of the Millennium Condominium. In 2006 the Senate launched an investigation into permit irregularities of the access to the San Jerónimo Fort as related to the construction of Paseo Caribe. In 2007 three more resolutions were passed to investigate the circumstances surrounding the permits process for the construction of Paseo Caribe. For a full legal and sociopolitical analysis of the controversy, see Érika Fontánez Torres and Mariana Muñiz Lara, "Derechos reales," *Revista Jurídica UPR* 79, no. 2 (2010): 472–510.

18. Roberto Sánchez Ramos, Consulta No. 7–130 B (Puerto Rico Department of Justice), https://www.yumpu.com/es/document/view/14159375/osj-2007-pc-opinion-sobre-titularidad-de-terrenos-lexjuris. See Fernós, *De San Jerónimo a Paseo Caribe*, 129–211, for the final report provided by the people's court.

19. On the findings, see https://www.scribd.com/document/26418736/Laudo-Interlocutorio-Tribunal-Del-Pueblo-Paseo-Caribe.

20. At the time, Luis Fortuño was the director of the company; he would later return to this issue as governor.

21. Puerta de Tierra was populated long before the Spanish arrived. For example, the site of the current National Guard Headquarters and

museum was originally the site of an indigenous village, probably an area used for fishing. Archaeologist Irving Rouse is credited with having identified remains of clay and rock utensils in the form of a shell (*conchero*) to locate several communities of indigenous peoples across the island. His work was concentrated in Haiti, but he spent several years early in his career in the late 1930s in Puerto Rico and exhumed approximately sixty-nine sites. See Irving Rouse, "New Evidence Pertaining to Puerto Rican Prehistory," *Proceedings of the National Academy of Sciences of the United States of America* 23, no. 3 (1937): 182–87, https://doi.org/10.1073/pnas .23.3.182. Rouse contributed to the myth of extinction of the Taino peoples so I mention his work with a healthy dose of skepticism. My desire is simply to note the presence of artefacts in PDT has long been acknowledged by researchers. In 2013 more studies were done to prevent further development. Although they were ultimately unsuccessful, their work validates the notion that there is a rich history of indigenous presence in the area. See, e.g., Sharon Melendez Ortiz, Samuel Márquez Santa, and Ruth M. García Pantaleón, "Evaluación Arqueológica Fase IA proyecto Paseo Lineal de Puerta de Tierra San Juan, Puerto Rico," December 2013, presented to Torres-Rosa Consulting Engineers, https://docplayer.es/7584416 -Evaluacion-arqueologica-fase-ia-proyecto-paseo-lineal-de-puerta-de -tierra-san-juan-puerto-rico.html.

22. Developers and government officials alike have wanted to empty PDT of its residents for years. In 1993 Luis Fortuño, then serving as director of the island's tourism company, included it in a plan called El Triángulo Dorado del Puerto de San Juan (Golden Triangle), unifying Condado and Old San Juan. Although the plan was first unveiled during the Pedro Rosselló administration it was not until 2009, when Fortuño was governor, that the plan was revived due to limited funds in the first iteration. Still, the plan for emptying PDT continued in the interim. In the early 2000s nearly a thousand families were pushed out because of the demolition of two public housing projects (La Acacia and PDT). Less than a hundred families returned when new buildings were finally erected. Government and private entities continued to chip away at the community in PDT. The next effort to "revitalize" the barrio came when the city built the PDT Promenade in 2015. The project consisted of constructing a bike lane adjacent to the ocean, as well as new pavements, seating areas, and green spaces built back into the cement promenade after the felling of hundreds of palm and pine trees that once lined the road. The promenade also included a restaurant, a ceramic mural, a sculpture, and a complete reorganization of the bus routes. This project was sold as an effort to make PDT more walkable

and cost a total of $32 million. By 2017 parts of the promenade were near collapse.

23. The Mendez brothers inherited the building from their grandfather who bought the property in the early 1900s, then just a small bodega and hardware store. He expanded eventually and built twenty-one residences above the store. Adjacent to the building was a large structure without roof used by the brothers mainly for storage and personal parking.

24. The link to his New York City profile is at https://www.linkedin.com /in/mayer-hazan-80916b58/; and his Puerto Rico profile at https://www .linkedin.com/in/mayer-hazan-311a551a7/.

25. In a little over a month, Hazan set up five different LLCs around San Juan. This is a common strategy mobilized by venture capitalists looking to secure their investments. They create different LLCs so that if they become enmeshed in a legal case, their other properties are not affected. Company Detail, *VMS Capital Group, Inc.*, https://www.company -detail.com/company-vms-capital-group-inc-4271738; Open Corporates, *MASSRI PR LLC*, https://opencorporates.com/companies?q=MASSRI+ PR+LLC&utf8=%E2%9C%93.

26. See Chiara De Cesari and Rozita Dimova "Heritage, Gentrification, Participation: Remaking Urban Landscapes in the Name of Culture and Historic Preservation," *International Journal of Heritage Studies* 25, no. 9 (2019): 863–69, https://doi.org/10.1080/13527258.2018.1512515.

27. The following are the reserves under attack: La Reserva Natural Finca Nolla, Reserva Agricola de la Costa Norte and Reserva Natural del Río Camuy, Reserva Natural Punta Cabullones, Reserva Natural Punta Guilarte, Reserva Natural Punta Petrona, Reserva Natural Mar Chiquita, Humedal de la Playa Lucía, and Reserva Natural Cañón San Cristobal. From the karst region where the majority of Puerto Rico's subterranean rivers live, the coast, and to agricultural lands key to fostering food sover-eignty and security in an archipelago that depends on the majority of its foods from import, the implications are immensely dark.

28. For a calculation of the percentage increase that Airbnb's existence causes on rent pricing more generally, see Kyle Barron, Edward Kung, and Davide Proserpio, "The Effect of Home-Sharing on House Prices and Rents," *Marketing Science* 40, no. 1 (2020): 23–47.

Microhistory 1

1. Hal Draper, "Towards a New Beginning: On Another Road" (1971), https://www.marxists.org/archive/draper/1971/alt/index.htm.

2. Like Comedores Sociales, the CAM model quickly spread across the island. At its height after Hurricane Maria, ten centers formed part of a loosely organized network. Although each CAM served food to its community, the programming and the direction of each group was shaped by the conditions and concerns of the communities they were based in.

3. *Comida pa' los Pobres* (*Food for the Poor*), directed by Arlene Cruz-Alicea (Research Triangle, NC: Reel South, 2021), https://www.pbs.org/vid eo/comida-pa-los-pobres-food-for-the-poor-n7pvba/?fbclid=IwAR3zpLohL PzjsTOSiI9ynQ1qOsp_NBzt1MDx4KIBgxJHjYl4umyuE7nJtfs.

Microhistory 2

1. *Parcelas* are plots of land that were given to landless Puerto Ricans by the government as part of the Land Reform Act of 1941. It was a redistribution effort to recapture the agricultural lands that were held by absentee owners, mainly US corporations, who had acquired land for sugar production in the years following the US occupation of Puerto Rico in 1898. While this government-sponsored project failed to massively redistribute lands, several land-owning communities across the island emerged of those who had been previously landless. For more information about the history of this program, see Ismael García-Colón, *Land Reform in Puerto Rico: Modernizing the Colonial State, 1941–1969* (Gainesville: University of Florida Press, 2009).

2. For more information about Las Nietas de Nonó's artistic work, visit their website https://www.lasnietasdenono.com.

3. These interviews were conducted in Spanish, but not all of my notes were in written in Spanish. Where possible, I will include the original Spanish.

4. Marianne Hirsch, "Family Pictures: *Maus*, Mourning and Post-Memory," *Discourse* 15, no. 2 (1992–93): 3–29.

5. One great example of this is the activist feminist press—Kitchen Table: Women of Color Press—cofounded in 1980 by Barbara Smith, Audre Lorde, Cherríe Moraga, Hattie Gossett, Helena Byard, Susan Yung, Ana Oliveira, Cherrie Moraga, Rosío Alvarez, Alma Gomez, and Leota Lone Dog. They chose to only publish works written by women of color. They saw the Kitchen Table as a place to disrupt the white-dominated media practice of refusing to print, reprint, and, in general, honor women of color by dedicating themselves to autonomously present and circulate works done by them.

Microhistory 3

1. For anyone unfamiliar with the history of Vieques, affectionately referred to as *la isla menor* (the little sister island), the US Navy used Vieques as a training range for "war games" for more than sixty years. Both ends of the island were occupied by the military, and the people lived in the middle. An intense period of direct action in the late 1990s and early 2000s caught the attention of high-profile international actors who helped provoke the end of the bombing. Despite the win, the military continues to avoid responsibility to clean up the contamination left behind by their war games. The bombing zone and the land used for storage of ammunition reserves were not returned to the people but were instead turned into the US's largest reserve. Currently, most of the island is under the management of the US government's wildlife and fishery department. As a result, the island is being sold as a site of "purity" to gringos who are buying the remaining land for their retirement and second winter homes, while the conditions of life for Viequenses worsen. For an in-depth exploration of these competing understandings of the island, see Sasha Davis, Jessica S. Hayes-Conroy, and Victoria M. Jones Davis, "Military Pollution and Natural Purity: Seeing Nature and Knowing Contamination in Vieques, Puerto Rico," *Geojournal* 69 (2017): 165–79.

2. These interviews were conducted in Spanish but not all of my notes were in written in Spanish. Where possible, I will include the original Spanish

3. For those unfamiliar, *jíbaro* is a term used in Puerto Rico to refer to people living in the mountainous regions of the island who maintained farming traditions and lived in relative isolation and autonomy from the state. During the rise to power of the island's first popularly elected governor, Luis Muñoz Marín, *the jíbaro* became a national icon and target of political intervention. Muñoz Marín broke with the tendency to dismiss *jíbaros* as ignorant and actively campaigned to poor people from the center of the island. In the process of turning this figure into an icon it was racially whitened. Even today a popular idea holds that *jíbaros* are whiter because they were isolated from the plantation economy instead of their more likely identity as indigenous and afro-indigenous people who escaped and evaded the plantation economy.

4. The 2018 census showed an overall decline in all these categories, with the exception of the age of farmers. In the under twenty-five age group, there was a sixty-percent-plus increase. US Census Bureau, *Agricultural Data Puerto Rico Release*, https://www.nass.usda.gov/Newsroom /Executive_Briefings/2020/06-09-2020.pdf.

5. Megan Horst and Amy Marion, "Racial, Ethnic and Gender Inequities in Farmland Ownership and Farming in the U.S.," *Agriculture and Human Values* 36 (2019): 1–16, https://doi.org/10.1007/s10460-018-9883-3.

6. Ivis Garcia, "The Lack of Proof of Ownership in Puerto Rico Is Crippling Repairs in the Aftermath of Hurricane Maria," *Human Rights Magazine* 44, no. 2 (May 21, 2021), https://www.americanbar.org/groups/crsj/publications/human_rights_magazine_home/vol--44--no-2--housing/the-lack-of-proof-of-ownership-in-puerto-rico-is-crippling-repai/.

7. For a fascinating full-length study of the complexities of land ownership, see Érika Fontánez Torres, *Casa suelo y título: Vivienda e informalidad en Puerto Rico* (San Juan, PR: Ediciones Laberinto, 2020).

8. Liliana Cotto, *Desalambrar: Origenes de los rescates de terreno en Puerto Rico y su pertinencia en los movimientos sociales contemporaneous* (San Juan, PR: Ediciones Tal Cual, 2006), 59–67.

Microhistory 4

1. *Okupa*, or squat, is a radical social movement with strong antecedents in Spain but visible throughout the world. Okupas are usually collective living arrangements within abandoned or unoccupied residences and offer an alternative to houselessness in the face of rising costs of rents and property speculation. This use of the particular spelling of "okupa" is meant to signal this project's connection with the social movement.

2. In 2020 Puerto Rico's civil code was revised. Articles 786 and 788 reduced the period of time necessary to acquire personal and real property through adverse possession. The acquisition of real property through adverse possession now requires at least ten years of possession in good faith and with color of title or at least twenty years of possession without. For further details on the changes made in 2020 to Puerto Rico's civil code, see Marcos Reyes Negrón, "Flexibilización de los requisitos de la prescripción adquisitiva inmobiliaria en Puerto Rico," *In Rev (la Revista Jurídica de la Universidad de Puerto Rico)*, https://revistajuridica.uprrp.edu/inrev/index.php/2020/11/05/flexibilizacion-de-los-requisitos-de-la-prescripcion-adquisitiva-inmobiliaria-en-puerto-rico/.

3. Centro de Recaudacion de Ingresos Municipales, or CRIM, is the government entity that taxes all property owners a yearly fee for their property. They also will maintain a record of debts that accrue over a period of time if an owner has abandoned said responsibilities for payment.

4. These are each of the definitions we coauthored for the principles that were operational in El Hormiguero.

1. Creemos en *la autogestión* como estrategia para transformar la sociedad desde abajo. Significa "hacerlo nosotros mismos," buscando autonomía y autosuficiencia. Partimos del reconocimiento de nuestras propias capacidades y recursos para administrar colectivamente los bienes y recursos materiales. Reivindicamos nuestra autonomía organizativa frente a la estructura estatal, movilizando redes de colaboradores y simpatizantes para propiciar la solidaridad entre nosotros/as y así propiciar el empoderamiento colectivo para el apoderamiento individual. 2. Creemos que *la solidaridad* es una práctica que lleva a cabo en el día a día con nuestra presencia. Sabemos que un sentido de colectividad entre los vecinos y nuestra okupa es necesario para fomentar *ubuntu*, término filosófico sudafricano de lengua zulu que significa "humanidad hacia otros." Entendemos que es vital que trabajemos a base de la convivencia social, ofreciendo la mano a aprender a solucionar problemas que son importantes para los que viven en la vecindad. Es a través del mundo cotidiano que cultivamos el sentido de humanidad. 3. Aspiramos a una sociedad verdaderamente *democrática, horizontal y participativa*. La supuesta democracia que vivimos cada cuatro años es una farsa. La llamada democracia representativa no nos representa, al contrario, nos impone desde arriba leyes injustas que atentan contra el bienestar de las mayorías. Por este motivo impulsamos la construcción de proyectos horizontales, es decir, organizaciones no jerárquicas donde la inclusión sea una parte fundamental de las mismas. La democracia que defendemos se da en espacios donde los y las participantes tienen la potestad de formar parte en los procesos de concepción de ideas, en la discusión y toma de decisiones y en su ejecución. Solo así lograremos una sana convivencia. Entendemos la horizontalidad como una forma alterna a las estructuras de control y participación empleados en la sociedad. Se busca promover una mejor convivencia a través de una democracia directa y prácticas inclusivas priorizando el fortalecimiento y autonomía de los individuos y organizaciones en una cultura solidaria.

(1) We believe in self-management as a strategy to transform society from below. It means "doing it ourselves," seeking autonomy and self-sufficiency. We start from the recognition of our own capacities and resources to collectively manage material goods and resources. We claim our autonomy from the state, mobilizing

networks of collaborators and allies to promote solidarity among ourselves and thus promote collective empowerment for individual empowerment. (2) We believe that *solidarity* is a practice that is enacted daily with our presence. We know that sense of collectivity between neighbors and our squat is necessary to foster *ubuntu*, a South African Zulu philosophical term meaning "humanity toward others." We understand that it is vital that we work on the basis of social coexistence, offering a hand in solving problems that are important to those who live in the neighborhood. It is through the everyday world that we cultivate a sense of humanity. (3) We aspire to a truly democratic, horizontal and participatory society. The democracy where we choose leadership every four years is a farce. The so-called representative democracy does not represent us; on the contrary, it imposes unjust laws from above that threaten the well-being of the majority. For this reason we promote the construction of horizontal projects, that is, nonhierarchical organizations where inclusion is a fundamental part of them. The democracy that we defend takes place in spaces where the participants have the power to take part in the processes of conception of ideas, in the discussion and decision making and in their execution. This is the only way to achieve a healthy coexistence. We understand horizontality as an alternative to the structures of control and participation used in society. We seek to promote a better coexistence through direct democracy and inclusive practices, prioritizing the strengthening and autonomy of individuals and organizations in a culture of solidarity.

5. Many thanks to Soul Fire Farm for their development of the courageous-conversation protocol. It was developed for their internal team as a way to give each other feedback regularly to avoid the build-up of resentments and to use any conflict as an opportunity to grow.

Microhistory 5

1. Generative Somatics, "Trauma, Healing and Collective Power," episode 1, June 2018. https://soundcloud.com/generativesomatics/trauma-healing-collective-power.

2. Agile learning is a powerful self-directed learning method developed to bolster student leadership and engagement. A flexible, student-led experience is what is prioritized by the model. Alex was certified as a trainer in

the methodology and his after school program, which has since closed was a part of an ALC network. Learn more at https://www.agilelearningcenters.org

Microhistory 6

1. Adela Nieves is the doula and *madrina* (godmother) of CEPA. She helped me to vision an early version of the project and was to rematriate with me, from her home in Detroit. Although it did not happen in the way we imagined, she has remained a close collaborator and supporter of CEPA.

2. Pat R. A., Lau (co-director CEPA), in discussion with the author, June 2021.

3. The word "batey" refers to a ceremonial plaza where Tainos gather for spiritual practice, and historically where a ball game *batú* was practiced.

4. When we began this project CEPA was exclusively a women's collective. We have evolved in our identity and thinking and so has the project. Still, it is central for us to both reclaim feminine energy, which has been so demonized and suppressed by Western society as we also make space for the healing of the masculine. Within patriarchy, we all have developed a damaged concept of masculinity and have held onto it to survive. None of this is simply about going back but about reclaiming to reimagine our lives.

5. For an excellent polemic on the use of the term "decolonization" as a synonym for improvement, see Tuck and Yang, *Decolonization: Indigeneity, Education & Society* 1, no. 1 (2012): 1–40.

6. Historically, palenques refer to communities of free people—usually composed of formerly enslaved black people and indigenous people living autonomously, and sometimes secretly, in the mountains. We see the name as a kind of inspiration and focus for population we want to populate these lands and the energy we hope to cultivate with this project.

Conclusion

1. Laura E. Pérez, "Enrique Dussel's *Etica de la liberación*: US Women of Color Decolonizing Practices and Coalitionary Politics Amidst Difference,".*Qui Parle*18, no. 2 (Spring/Summer 2010): 121–46.

2. In *Emergent Strategy: Shaping Change, Changing Worlds* (Chico, CA: AK Press, 2017), adrienne maree brown works directly with Octavia Butler's principles as present in her 1993 speculative fiction novel *Parable of the Sower*.

3. Tropicolonia is a colloquial and irreverent way to refer to the inefficiencies of the system of governance in PR (a colony) within the geographical context of the Caribbean (tropical).

Coda

1. Sarah Ihmoud, "Love in a Time of Genocide: A Palestinian Litany for Survival," *Journal of Palestine Studies* 52, no. 4 (2023): 87–94, doi:10.1080 /0377919X.2023.2289363; Devin Atallah and Nihaya Abu-Rayyan, "There is no lifting the rubble from afar: A conversation between two Palestinian healers waging love against genocide," Palestine Square (blog), Institute for Palestine Studies, January 31, 2024, https://www.palestine-studies.org /en/node/1655131.

2. Tricia Hersey, *Rest is Resistance: A Manifesto* (New York: Little Brown Spark, 2022), 165

3. Rosa Amelia Giove Nakazawa is often credited as the author of this *ícaro*, or ritual song, but I was not able to find a official release of the song by her. Giove was a doctor and researcher of addiction and the treatment of it by ancestral plants from the Amazon. The song was later popularized and released by Alonso del Río's album *Punto de Fase* in 2001.

4. The technical or more literal translations "la jornada" workshop, meeting, a period of working hours or days don't fully explain the nature of the gathering. Yes, there are workshops, led mainly but not exclusively by indigenous elders. But there is also ceremony, which may be for me, the most important part of the gathering. We also camp on the grounds of Coabey in connection with this field of ancestral presence wisdom. To honor the complexities, and lack of translatability of the term, I will maintain use of *la jornada*.

5. Jamie Sams, *Sacred Path Cards: The Discovery of Self Through Native Teachings* (San Francisco: HarperCollins, 1990). Although this tarot deck may be a nontraditional source for a book, I think it's a great entryway for anyone beginning a reclamation journey and wanting to learn a pan-indigenous perspective on spiritual practice and self-discovery. The work of connecting to one's lineage and specific ancestral cosmology, stories, and teachings is much more complex, but it's a playful place to explore.

6. Learn more about Veronica's work at http://www.veronicaagard.com /ancestors-in-training.

7. Ana Portnoy Brimmer, *To Love an Island* (Portland, OR: YesYes Books, 2021), 1–4.

8. Special thank you to Qiddist Ashé, a clinical herbalist, certified childbirth educator, and birth worker, for her teachings on energetic sovereignty. To learn more about her work, visit https://thewombroom.co.

9. Frenak, *Ancestral Future*, 12.

10. In the appendix I have included a guide Lau Pat R.A. and I cowrote in 2019 to set the tone for participants in CEPA's pilot network formation. In our efforts to bring together healers and artists working together for healing justice in and across the archipelago and diaspora, we got clear on some important distinctions, and this was our first attempt to name them.

11. Tracking the immensity of this support is difficult. I do not know of a study that attempted to quantify the aid we received from our diaspora kin. Diaspora-based Boricuas did everything they could. Some held community drives, organized fundraisers, and more. Those who had access to foundations created special funds. My family and close friends sent food that was not readily available directly to us, and others flew in generators and medicine—any and everything you can imagine. We received hundreds of boxes of medicine and medical supplies from as far away as Hawai'i all based on the work of two Boricuas in the diaspora. Thank you Eroc Arroyo and Adela Nieves Martinez. I cannot imagine what the experience would have been like without this support. These efforts are discussed in two articles: Jeremy Deaton "Puerto Rico Still Needs Help: These People Picked up the Cost," *Peril and Promise: The Challenges of Climate Change*, May 17, 2019, https://www.pbs.org/wnet/peril-and-promise/2019/05/puerto-rico-still-needs-help-these-people-picked-up-the-cost/; and David Gonzales, "On the Mainland, a Duty to Help Puerto Rico," *New York Times*, October 29, 2017, https://www.nytimes.com/2017/10/29/nyregion/on-the-mainland-a-duty-to-help-puerto-rico.html.

12. Rebecca Solnit, *A Paradise Built in Hell: The Extraordinary Communities That Arise in Disaster* (Westminster, London: Penguin Press, 2010).

13. Many thanks to Xiomara Caro who helped to shape this analysis with me in conversations we had poststorm. These observations led to us organizing a delegation of activists to visit Detroit during the 2018 Allied Media Conference. During that time we organized meetups with other Black and Brown activists to talk about the challenges of shifting from allyship to coconspiration and the need to integrate healing into our movement work. These were times of deep sharing, restorative practice, movement and celebration. More information about the delegation including biographies of participants can be found at https://docs.google.com/document/d/1R9pgEPJk1t_oG1Yg8u-Qv4uae82JW67rCYGL94VxfNY/edit.

14. Leanne Betasamosake Simpson, *Islands of Decolonial Love* (Winnipeg, ON: ARP Books, 2013). "still, i am not tragic" is the epigraph that opens the book from the poem "Blind Justice" by Lee Maracle published in *Decolonization: Indigeneity, Education & Society* 2, no. 1 (2013): 134–36.

15. From a speech given by adrienne maree brown at a meeting of the Embodiment Institute, "Gather: A Celebration with the Embodiment Institute Team," Durham, North Carolina, September 9, 2023.

16. Ana Portnoy Brimmer, *To Love an Island* (Portland, OR: YesYes Books, 2021), 1–4.

17. Many thanks to Alice Baca for her work on this concept. She is the founder and editor of the magazine *Life as Ceremony*, an independent biannual print journal that centers indigenous and black folx, communities of color, the LGBTQIA community, and those otherwise marginalized, erased, or forgotten. Learn more at https://lifeasceremony.wixsite.com /lifeasceremony.

Appendix

1. This is a revised version of a document that Lau Pat R.A. and I coauthored when we first piloted the network formation of CEPA. It was meant to be a starting point for all CEPA collaborators to reflect on what it means to be in solidarity across geographic locations and positions. I have made some small changes to make it legible within the context of a book publication.

2. Paolo Freire's *Pedagogy of the Oppressed* speaks directly to this conundrum. "Solidarity requires that one enters into the situation of those with whom one is in solidarity [and] means fighting at their side to transform the objective reality." Paolo Freire, *Pedagogy of the Oppressed*, trans. Maya Bergman Ramos (1970; New York. Continuum Press: 2005), 49.

3. "Cross-charco" is a term I first heard used by Yasmin Hernandez, fellow rematriator and artist. To jump the pond, or brincar el charco, is a common phrasing within migrating people in the Puerto Rican community. Cross-charco, then, refers to the ocean as charco, or pond, and to us being in relationship across it.

4. The consistent comings and goings of Boris have been explored in many mediums. See, for example, Alanis Santiago-Rodriguez's short film *El Vaivén*, https://www.alanissantiagorodriguez.com/elvaiven, and Alana Casanova-Burgess's "Embracing the Vaivén in Puerto Rican Reporting," NACLA, December 9, 2021, https://nacla.org/news/2021/12/09/la-brega -puerto-rico.

5. See Romesh Hettiarachchi's "Diaspora Responsibilities: The (Mis)
Conception of Diaspora Privilege," published on November 9, 2013, in
the *Colombo Telegraph*, https://www.colombotelegraph.com/index.php
/diaspora-responsibilities-the-misconception-of-diaspora-privilege/,   and
Yasmin Hernandez's "Repatriation: Critical Concept Missing in Relief
Efforts," *La Respuesta*.

BIBLIOGRAPHY

Acosta, Roland, Nishant Kishore, Rafael Irizarry, and Caroline Bucknee. "Quantifying the Dynamics of Migration after Hurricane Maria in Puerto Rico." *Proceedings of the National Academy of Sciences* 117, no. 51 (2020): 32772–8.

Aldarondo, Cecilia. *Landfall*. Blackscrackle Films, 2020.

Anzaldúa, Gloria. *Borderlands/La Frontera: The New Mestiza*. San Francisco: Aunt Lute Press, 1987.

Aronoff, Kate. "Armed Federal Agents Enter Warehouse in Puerto Rico to Seize Hoarded Electric Equipment." *Intercept*, January 10, 2018. https://theintercept.com/2018/01/10/puerto-rico-electricity-prepa-hurricane-maria/.

Atallah, Devin, and Nihaya Abu-Rayyan. "There is no lifting the rubble from afar: A conversation between two Palestinian healers waging love against genocide" Palestine Square (blog), Institute for Palestine Studies, January 31, 2024. https://www.palestine-studies.org/en/node/1655131.

Bambara, Toni Cade, ed. *The Black Woman: An Anthology*. New York: New American Library, 1970.

Barron, Kyle, Edward Kung, and Davide Proserpio. "The Effect of Home-Sharing on House Prices and Rents: Evidence from Airbnb." *Marketing Science* 40, no.1 (2020): 23–47.

Benedetti, María. *Árboles nuestros para la supervivencia*. Bogotá, Colombia: Nomos, 2019.

Bernabe, Rafael, and Cesar Ayala. *Puerto Rico in the American Century: A History Since 1898*. Durham, NC: Duke University Press, 2007.

Black, Stephanie. dir. *Life and Debt*. London: Axiom Films, 2001.

Bonilla, Yarimar. "The Swarm of Disaster." *Political Geography* 84 (2020): 1–3. https://doi.org/10.1016/j.polgeo.2020.102182.

Bonilla, Yarimar, and Marisol Lebrón. *Aftershocks of Disaster: Puerto Rico Before and After the Storm*. New York: Haymarket Press, 2019.

Bonilla, Yarimar, Rima Brusi, and Natasha Lycia Ora Bannan. "6 Months after Maria, Puerto Ricans Face a New Threat—Education Reform."

Nation, March 21, 2018. https://www.thenation.com/article/archive
/colonialism-and-disaster-capitalism-are-dismantling-puerto-ricos
-public-school-system/.

brown, adrienne maree. *Emergent Strategy: Shaping Change, Changing Worlds*. Chico, CA: AK Press, 2017.

Brown, Nick. "Puerto Rico's Other Crisis: Impoverished Pensions." *Reuters: Uneasy Island Series*, April 7, 2016. https://www.reuters.com/investigates /special-report/usa-puertorico-pensions/.

Cáez, Giovanni Roberto. "Huelga 2017 en la mirada del CUCA 2005." Centro para el Desarrollo Político, Educativo y Cultural, April 20, 2019. https://www.cdpecpr.org/single-post/huelga-2017-en-la-mirada-del-cuca -2005. Accessed June 29, 2019.

Castanha, Tony. *The Myth of Indigenous Caribbean Extinction*. New York: Palgrave Macmillan, 2010.

Center for Investigative Journalism Team. "Gobierno pide mantener en sobre sellado y guardado en una bóveda el informe sobre el almacén de suministros." Centro de Periodismo Investigativo, March 5, 2020. https://peri odismoinvestigativo.com/2020/03/en-sobre-sellado-y-guardado-en-una-bo veda-del-tribunal-el-informe-sobre-el-almacen-de-suministros-en-ponce/.

Center for Investigative Journalism Team. "Gobierno entrega a la prensa informe de almacén de suministros." Centro de Periodismo Investigativo, March 13, 2020. https://periodismoinvestigativo.com/2020/03/gobierno -entrega-a-la-prensa-informe-de-almacen-de-suministros/.

Chavez, Nicole, and Rafy Rivera. "Puerto Rico Emergency Director Fired after Residents Discover Warehouse Full of Hurricane Maria Supplies." *CNN*, January 19, 2020. https://edition.cnn.com/2020/01/18/us/puerto -rico-emergency-director-fired/index.html.

Clemente, Yaritza Rivera. "Aprueban resolución oponiéndose al recorte a las pensiones y al Plan de Ajuste." *El Vocero*, October 21, 2019. https://www .elvocero.com/gobierno/aprueban-resoluci-n-oponi-ndose-al-recorte -a-las-pensiones-y-al-plan-de-ajuste/article_2190b716-f43c-11e9-a6e8 -97c15d2d0148.html.

Combahee River Collective. *The Combahee River Collective Statement: Black Feminist Organizing in the Seventies and Eighties*. Albany, NY: Kitchen Table Women of Color Press, 1986.

Company Detail. *VMS Capital Group, INC*. Retrieved June 19, 2020. https://www.company-detail.com/company-vms-capital-group-inc -4271738.

Cordero, Mikey, dir. *The War against Our Schools: Defending Public Education in Puerto Rico*. Carolina: Defend Puerto Rico, 2021.

Corsín Jimenez, Alberto, and Adolfo Estalella. "The Atmospheric Person: Value, Experiment, and Making Neighbors in Madrid's Popular Assemblies." *HAU: Journal of Ethnographic Theory* 3, no. 2 (2013): 119–39.

Cotto, Liliana. *Desalambrar: Origenes de los rescates de terreno en Puerto Rico y su pertinencia en los movimientos sociales contemporaneos.* San Juan, PR: Ediciones Tal Cual, 2006.

Cotto-Quijano, Evaluz. "How the Triple Tax Exemption on Puerto Rico's Bonds Financed Its Territorial Status—and Helped Spark Its Debt Crisis." *Promarket*, September 11, 2018. https://promarket.org/triple-tax-exemption-puerto-ricos-bonds-financed-territorial-status-helped-spark-debt-crisis/.

Cruz-Alicea, Arlene, dir. *Comida pa' los Pobres (Food for the Poor).* PBS North Carolina (Research Triangle, NC): PBS Reel South Series, 2021.

Dávila Santiago, Juan C., dir. *La generacion del estanbi (The Stand-by Generation).* New York: Third World Newsreel, 2015.

Davis, Sasha, Jessica S. Hayes-Conroy, and Victoria M. Jones. "Military Pollution and Natural Purity: Seeing Nature and Knowing Contamination in Vieques, Puerto Rico." *Geojournal* 69, no. 3 (2007): 165–79.

Deaton, Jeremy. "Puerto Rico Still Needs Help: These People Picked up the Cost." *Peril and Promise: The Challenges of Climate Change*, May 17, 2019. https://www.pbs.org/wnet/peril-and-promise/2019/05/puerto-rico-still-needs-help-these-people-picked-up-the-cost/.

De Cesari, Chiara, and Rozita Dimova. "Heritage, Gentrification, Participation: Remaking Urban Landscapes in the Name of Culture and Historic Preservation." *International Journal of Heritage Studies* 25, no. 9 (2019): 863–69. https://doi.org/10.1080/13527258.2018.1512515.

Dennis, Abner. "COVID-19 and the Collapse of Private Hospitals in Puerto Rico." LittleSis, April 9, 2020. https://news.littlesis.org/2020/04/09/covid-19-and-the-collapse-of-private-hospitals-in-puerto-rico/.

Dick, Diane Lourdes. "US Tax imperialism in Puerto Rico." *American University Law Review* 65, no. 1 (2015): 1–87.

Dietz, James L. *Economic History of Puerto Rico: Institutional Change and Capitalist Development.* Princeton, NJ: Princeton University Press, 1986.

Dinzey-Flores, Zaire Zenit. *Locked In, Locked Out: Gated Communities in a Puerto Rican City* Philadelphia: University of Pennsylvania, 2013.

Draper, Hal. "Towards a New Beginning: On Another Road" (1971). https://www.marxists.org/archive/draper/1971/alt/index.htm.

Duany, Jorge. *The Puerto Rican Nation on the Move: Identities on the Island and in the United States*. Durham, NC: University of North Carolina, 2002.

Dubois, Laurent. *Haiti: The Aftershocks of History*. London: Picador Press, 2012.

Duffy Burnett, Christina, and Burke Marshall. *Foreign in a Domestic Sense: Puerto Rico, American Expansion and the Constitution*. Durham, NC: Duke University Press, 2001.

Everhart, Katherine. "Cultura-Identidad: The Use of Art in the University of Puerto Rico Student Movement, 2010." *Humanity & Society* 36, no. 3 (2012): 198–219.

Fernòs, Antonio. *De San Jerónimo a Paseo Caribe*. San Juan, PR: Ediciones Puerto: 2008.

Figueroa Huertas, Verónica. "Intervención femenina en la huelga 2017: Más allá de rostros y números." *Diálogo*, April 1, 2018. https://dialogo .upr.edu/intervencion-femenina-en-la-huelga-2017-mas-alla-de-rostros -y-numeros/.

Fontánez Torres, Érika. *Casa suelo y título: Vivienda e informalidad en Puerto Rico*. San Juan, PR: Ediciones Laberinto, 2020.

Fontánez Torres, Érika, and Marina Muñiz Lara. "Derechos reales." *Revista Jurídica UPR* 79, no. 2 (2010): 472–510.

Frenak, Ailton. *Ancestral Future*. Edited by Rita Carelli. Translation. Alex Brostoff and Jamille Pinheiro Dias. Cambridge Polity Press, 2024.

Frontline. "How Banks Responded to 'Blackout in Puerto Rico.'" PBS, May 1, 2018. https://www.pbs.org/wgbh/frontline/article/how-banks -responded-to-blackout-in-puerto-rico/.

Garcia, Ivis. "The Lack of Proof of Ownership in Puerto Rico Is Crippling Repairs in the Aftermath of Hurricane Maria." *Human Rights Magazine* 44, no. 2 (May 21, 2021). https://www.americanbar.org /groups/crsj/publications/human_rights_magazine_home/vol--44--no-2 --housing/the-lack-of-proof-of-ownership-in-puerto-rico-is-crippling -repai/.

García-Colón, Ismael. *Land Reform in Puerto Rico: Modernizing the Colonial State, 1941–1969*. Gainesville: University of Florida Press, 2009.

Garriga-López, Adriana María. "Debt Crisis and Resurgence in Puerto Rico." *Small Axe* 24, no. 2 (July 2020): 122–32.

Generative Somatics. "Trauma, Healing and Collective Power." Episode 1, June 2018. https://soundcloud.com/generativesomatics/trauma-healing -collective-power.

Georas, Cloe. "Native of Nowhere." In *Puerto Rican Jam: Rethinking Colonialism and Nationalism*, edited by Frances Negrón-Muntaner and Ramon Grosfoguel, iv–xi. Minneapolis: University of Minnesota Press, 1997.

Godreau-Aubert, Ariadna. *Las propias: Apuntes para una pedagogía de las endeudadas*. San Juan, PR: Ediciones Emergentes, 2017.

Goldman, Danielle. *I Want to Be Ready: Improvised Dance as a Practice of Freedom*. Ann Arbor: University of Michigan Press, 2010.

Goldstein, Aloysha. "Promises Are Over: Puerto Rico and the Ends of Decolonization." *Theory & Event* 19, no. 4 (2016): 1–14.

Gómez-Barris, Macarena. *The Extractive Zone: Social Ecologies and Decolonial Perspectives*. Durham, NC: Duke University Press 2017.

Gonzalez, David. "On the Mainland, a Duty to Help Puerto Rico." *New York Times*, October 29, 2017. https://www.nytimes.com/2017/10/29/nyregion/on-the-mainland-a-duty-to-help-puerto-rico.html.

Gonzalez, Juan. "Puerto Rico's Economic 'Death Spiral' Tied to Legacy of Colonialism." *Democracy Now*, August 5, 2015. https://www.democracynow.org/2015/8/5/juan_gonzalez_puerto_ricos_economic_death.

Gordon, Lewis. *Freedom and Power in the Caribbean*. New York City: Monthly Review Press, 1975.

Gould, Deborah B. *Moving Politics: Emotion and ACT UP's Fight Against AIDS*. Chicago: University of Chicago Press, 2009.

Graeber, David. *Debt: The First 5,000 Years*. London: Melville House, 2011.

Griffin, Susan. *A Chorus of Stones: The Private Life of War*. New York: Anchor Books, 1992.

Guattari, Félix, and Gilles Deleuze. *Capitalism and Schizophrenia*. Translated by R. Hurley, M. Seem, and H. R. Lane. New York: Viking Press, 1977.

Harney, Stefano, and Fred Moten. *Undercommons: Fugitive Planning and Black Study*. London: Minor Compositions, 2013.

Hedge Clippers and the Committee for Better Banks. "Pirates of the Caribbean: How Santander's Revolving Door with Puerto Rico's Development Bank Exacerbated a Fiscal Catastrophe for the Puerto Rican People." *Hedge Papers*, December 13, 2016. http://hedgeclippers.org/wp-content/uploads/2016/12/20161025_HedgeClippers_ReportPR_v3-3.pdf.

Hersey, Tricia. *Rest Is Resistance: A Manifesto*. New York: Little Brown Spark, 2022.

Hinojosa, Jennifer, and Edwin Meléndez. "The Housing Crisis in Puerto Rico and the Impact of Hurricane Maria." Center for Puerto Rican Studies,

Hunter College, June 2018. https://issuu.com/coleccionpuertorriquena/docs/housingpuertorico.

Hinojosa, Jennifer, Edwin Meléndez, and Kathya Severino Pietri. "Population Decline and School Closure in Puerto Rico." Center for Puerto Rican Studies, Hunter College, May 14, 2019. https://centropr.hunter.cuny.edu/sites/default/files/PDF_Publications/centro_rb2019-01_cor.pdf. Accessed September 18, 2019.

Hirsch, Marianne. "Family Pictures: *Maus,* Mourning and Post-Memory." *Discourse* 15, no. 2 (1992–93): 3–29.

Holloway, John. *Change the World without Taking Power: The Meaning of Revolution Today.* London: Pluto Press, 2003.

hooks, bell. *Ain't I a Woman? Black Women and Feminism.* Boston: South End Press, 1981.

Horst, Megan, and Amy Marion. "Racial, Ethnic and Gender Inequities in Farmland Ownership and Farming in the U.S." *Agriculture and Human Values* 36 (2019): 1–16. https://doi.org/10.1007/s10460-018-9883-3.

Ihmoud, Sarah. 2023. "Love in a Time of Genocide: A Palestinian Litany for Survival." *Journal of Palestine Studies* 52 (4): 87–94. doi:10.1080/0377919X.2023.2289363.

Juris, Jeffrey, and Maple Rasza. "Occupy, Anthropology, and the 2011 Global Uprisings." Hot Spots, *Fieldsights,* July 27, 2012. https://culanth.org/fieldsights/series/occupy-anthropology-and-the-2011-global-uprisings.

Kishora, Nishant, Domingo Marqués, Ayesha Mahmud, Mathew V. Kiang, Imary Rodriguez, Arlan Fuller, Peggy Ebner, Cecilia Sorensen, Fabio Racy, Jay Lemery, Leslie Mass, Jennifer Leaning, et. al. "Mortality in Puerto Rico after Hurricane Maria." *New England Journal of Medicine* 379 (2018): 162–70. https://doi.org/10.1056/NEJMsa1803972.

Klein, Naomi. *The Battle for Paradise: Puerto Rico Takes on the Disaster Capitalists.* Translated by Teresa Córdova Rodríguez. Chicago: Haymarket Books, 2018.

Klein, Naomi. *The Shock Doctrine: The Rise of Disaster Capitalism.* Toronto: Knopf Canada, 2007.

Kobes, Deborah Isadora. "Out of Control? Local Democracy Failure and Fiscal Control Boards." PhD diss., Massachusetts Institute of Technology, 2009.

Krugman, Paul. "The Case for Cuts Was a Lie. Why Does Britain Still Believe It? The Austerity Delusion." *Guardian,* April 29, 2015. https://www.theguardian.com/business/ng-interactive/2015/apr/29/the-austerity-delusion.

Lamba-Nieves, Deepak, Sergio M. Marxuach, and Rosanna Torres. "PROMESA: A Failed Colonial Experiment?" *Center for a New Economy* 7–8 (June 2021). https://grupocne.org/wp-content/uploads/2021/06 /2021.06.29-PROMESA-A-Failed-Colonial-Experiment.pdf.

LeBrón, Marisol. *Against Muerto Rico: Lessons from the Verano Boricua.* Cabo Rojo, PR: Editora Educación Emergente, 2021.

Lorde, Audre. *Sister Outsider: Essays and Speeches.* Berkeley, CA: Crossing Press, 1984.

Maharawal, Manissa. "Occupy Wall Street and a Racial Politics of Inclusion." *Sociological Quarterly* 54, no. 2 (2013): 177–81.

Maldonado Torres, Nelson. "Outline of Ten Theses on Coloniality and Decoloniality." http://caribbeanstudiesassociation.org/docs/Maldonado -Torres_Outline_Ten_Theses-10.23.16.pdf.

Martínez-Cruzado, Juan C., Gladys Toro-Labrador, Jorge Viera-Vera, Michelle Y. Rivera-Vega, Jennifer Startek, Magda Latorre-Esteves, Alicia Román-Colón, et al. "Reconstructing the Population History of Puerto Rico by Means of mtDNA Phylogeographic Analysis." *American Journal of Physical Anthropology* 128, no. 1 (2005): 131–55. doi.org/10.1002 /ajpa.20108. Accessed September 18, 2019.

Martínez Mercado, Eliván. 2012. "Las fincas fantasma de Santini." Centro de Periodismo Investigativo, November 2, 2012. https:// periodismoinvestigativo.com/2012/11/las-fincas-fantasma-de-santini/.

Melendez Ortiz, Sharon, Samuel Márquez Santa, and Ruth M. García Pantaleón. "Evaluación Arqueológica Fase IA proyecto Paseo Lineal de Puerta de Tierra San Juan, Puerto Rico." December 2013. https:// docplayer.es/7584416-Evaluacion-arqueologica-fase-ia-proyecto-paseo -lineal-de-puerta-de-tierra-san-juan-puerto- rico.html.

McCormick, Kate, and Emma Schwartz. "After Maria, Thousands on Puerto Rico Waited Months for a Plastic Roof." *Frontline*, May 2, 2018. https://www.pbs.org/wgbh/frontline/article/after-maria-thousands-on -puerto-rico-waited-months-for-a-plastic-roof.

Minet, Carla. "Papelón tras papelón en el caso del almacén de Ponce." Centro de Periodismo Investigativo, March 8, 2020. https:// periodismoinvestigativo.com/2020/03/papelon-tras-papelon-en-el-caso -del-almacen-de-ponce/.

Minh-ha, Trinh T. *Woman, Native, Other: Writing Postcoloniality and Feminism.* Indianapolis: Indiana University Press, 1989.

Moraga, Cherríe. "An Irrevocable Promise: Staging the Story Xicana." In *Radical Acts: Theatre and Feminist Pedagogies of Change*, edited by

Ann Elizabeth Armstrong and Kathleen Juhl. San Francisco: Aunt Lute Books, 2007: 34-46.

Morales, Ed. *Fantasy Island: Colonialism, Exploitation, and the Betrayal of Puerto Rico*. New York: Bold Type Books, 2019.

Moten, Fred. *In the Break: The Aesthetics of the Black Radical Tradition*. Minneapolis: University of Minnesota Press, 2003.

Namerrow, Lale. "Puerto Rico Summer Uprising: What Comes Next?" Hemispheric Institute, New York University, November 18, 2019. https://hemisphericinstitute.org/en/events/puerto-rico-summer-uprising.html.

Navarro-Rivera, Pablo. "Acculturation under Duress: The Puerto Rican Experience at the Carlisle Indian Industrial School 1898–1918." *Centro Journal* 18, no. 1 (2006): 222–59.

Negron-Muntaner, Frances. "The Emptying Island: Puerto Rican Expulsion in Post-Maria Time." *Emisferica* 14, no. 1 (2018). https://hemisphericinstitute.org/en/emisferica-14-1-expulsion/14-1-essays/the-emptying-island-puerto-rican-expulsion-in-post-maria-time.html.

Nieves Falcón, Luis, and Ineke Cunningham y Israel Rivera. *Huelga y sociedad: Analisis de los sucesos en la UPR, 1981–1982*. Río Piedras, PR: Editorial Edil, 1982.

Nixon, Angelique V. *Resisting Paradise: Tourism, Diaspora and Sexuality in Caribbean Culture*. Jackson: University Press of Mississippi, 2015.

Page, Cara. "Reflections from Detroit: Transforming Wellness and Wholeness." *INCITE!* August 5, 2010. https://incite-national.org/2010/08/05/reflections-from-Detroit-transforming-wellness-wholeness/.

Page, Cara, and Erica Woodland. *Healing Justice Lineages: Dreaming at the Crossroads of Liberation, Collective Care and Safety*. Berkeley, CA: North Atlantic Books, 2023.

Pérez Ramos, José G., Adriana Garriga-López, and Carlos E. Rodríguez-Díaz. "How Is Colonialism a Sociostructural Determinant of Health in Puerto Rico?" *AMA Journal of Ethics* 24, no. 4 (2022): E305–12. https://doi.org/10.1001/amajethics.2022.305.

Piepzna-Samarasinha, Leah Lakshmi. "A Not-So-Brief Personal History of the Healing Justice Movement, 2010–2016." *Mice Magazine*. https://micemagazine.ca/issue-two/not-so-brief-personal-history-healing-justice-movement-2010–2016.

Open Corporates. *MASSRI PR LLC*. Retrieved June 10, 2020. https://opencorporates.com/companies?q=MASSRI+PR+LLC&utf8=%E2%9C%93.

Park, Stephen, and Tim R. Samples. "Puerto Rico's Debt Dilemma and Pathways toward Sovereign Solvency" (January 27, 2017). *American Business Law Journal* 54, no. 1 (2017). https://ssrn.com/abstract=2826301.

Portnoy Brimmer, Ana. *To Love an Island*. Portland, OR: YesYes Books, 2021.

Ponder, C. S. "Cuando Colón baje el dedo: The Role of Repair in Urban Reproduction." *Urban Geography* 44, no. 9 (2023): 1853–73.

Quashie, Kevin. *Black Aliveness, or A Poetics of Being*. Durham, NC: Duke University Press, 2021.

Renta, Natalie, Maggie Corser, and Saqib Bhatti. "PROMESA Has Failed: How a Colonial Board Is Enriching Wall Street and Hurting Puerto Ricans." Center for Popular Democracy, September 2021. https://www.populardemocracy.org/PROMESAHasFailed.

Reyes Negrón, Marcos R. "Flexibilización de los requisitos de la prescripción adquisitiva inmobiliaria en Puerto Rico." *In Rev (Revista Jurídica de la Universidad de Puerto Rico)*, November 5, 2020. https://derecho.uprrp.edu/inrev/2020/11/05/flexibilizacion-de-los-requisitos-de-la-prescripcion-adquisitiva-inmobiliaria-en-puerto-rico/.

Robles, Frances. "The Lineman Got $63 an Hour: The Utility was Billed $100." *New York Times*, November 12, 2017. https://www.nytimes.com/2017/11/12/us/whitefish-energy-holdings-prepa-hurricane-recovery-corruption-hurricane-recovery-in-puerto-rico.html.

Rosario, Melissa. "Ephemeral Spaces, Undying Dreams: Social Justice Struggles in Contemporary Puerto Rico." PhD diss., Cornell University, 2013.

Rosario, Melissa. "Inhabiting the Aporias of Empire: Protest Politics in Contemporary Puerto Rico." In *Ethnographies of US Empire*, edited by Carole McGranahan and John F. Collins, 112–28. Durham, NC: Duke University Press, 2018.

Rosario, Melissa. "Intimate Publics: Autoethnographic Meditations on the Micropolitics of Resistance." *Anthropology and Humanism* 39, no. 1 (2014): 36–54.

Rosario, Melissa. "Public Pedagogy in the Creative Strike: Destabilizing Boundaries and Reimagining Resistance in the University of Puerto Rico." *Curriculum Inquiry* 45, no. 1 (2015): 52–68.

Rouse, Irving. "New Evidence Pertaining to Puerto Rican Prehistory." *Proceedings of the National Academy of Sciences of the United States of America* 23, no. 3 (1937): 182–18. https://doi.org/10.1073/pnas.23.3.182.

Salas Rivera, Raquela. *lo terciario / the tertiary*. Blacksbury, VA: Noemi Press, 2019.

Sánchez Ramos, Roberto. *Consulta No. 7–130 B*. Puerto Rico Department of Justice. https://www.yumpu.com/es/document/view/14159375/osj-2007-pc-opinion-sobre-titularidad-de-terrenos-lexjuris.

Santiago Ortiz, Aurora. "Testimonia as Stitch Work: Undoing Coloniality Through Autoethnography in Puerto Rico." *Chicana/Latina Studies: The Journal of Mujeres Activas en Letras y Cambio Social* 20, no. 2 (2021): 122–48.

Schuller, Mark. *Humanity's Last Stand: Confronting Global Catastrophe*. New Brunswick, NJ: Rutgers University, 2021.

Schwartz, Emma. "FEMA Tarp Contractor under Investigation for Fraud." *Frontline*, June 14, 2019. https://www.pbs.org/wgbh/frontline/article/fema-tarp-contractor-under-investigation-for-fraud/.

Serrano Román, Angélica. "Public Schools in Puerto Rico with No Resources to Comply with Vocational Evaluations for Students with Special Needs." Centro de Periodismo Investigativo, February 13, 2020. https://periodismoinvestigativo.com/2020/02/public-schools-in-puerto-rico-with-no-resources-to-comply-with-vocational-evaluations-for-students-with-special- needs/.

Sheller, Mimi. *Island Futures: Caribbean Survival in the Anthropocene*. Durham, NC: Duke University Press, 2 2020.

Simpson, Leanne B. *Islands of Decolonial Love: Stories and Songs*. Winnipeg, ON: ARP Books, 2013.

Slavin, Robert. "Puerto Rico Oversight Board Sues Governor, Legislature." *Bond Buyer*, July 2, 2021. https://www.bondbuyer.com/news/puerto-rico-oversight-board-sues-governor-legislature.

Solman, Paul. "America's Best Kept Financial Secret: I Bonds." *Making Sen$e*, October 11, 2012. https://www.pbs.org/newshour/economy/americas-best-kept-financial-secret-i-bonds.

Solnit, Rebecca. *A Paradise Built in Hell: The Extraordinary Communities That Arise in Disaster*. Westminster: London Penguin Press, 2010.

Solomon, Clare, and Tania Palmieri, eds. *Springtime: The New Student Rebellions*. Brooklyn, NY: Verso Press, 2011.

Stanchich, Maritza. "University Besieged: Dimensions, Contexts, Stakes" *Sargasso* no. 1 (2011–12): ix–xxxi. http://humanidades.uprrp.edu/ingles./pdfs/sargasso/TOC2011-2012,%20I.pdf. Accessed May 30, 2015.

Tuck, Eve, and K. Wayne Yang. "Decolonization Is Not a Metaphor." *Decolonization: Indigeneity, Education & Society* 1, no. 1 (2012): 1–40.

Ulysse, Gina. *Why Haiti Needs New Narratives: A Post-Quake Chronicle*. Middletown, CT: Wesleyan University Press, 2015.

Uperesa, Fáanofo Lisaclaire, and Adriana Garriga-Lopez. "Contested Sovereignties: Puerto Rico and America Samoa." In *Sovereign Acts: Contesting Colonialism Across Indigenous Nations and Latinx America*, ed. Frances Negron-Muntaner, 39–81. Tucson: University of Arizona Press, 2017.

US Department of Agriculture, National Agricultural Statistics Service. *2018 Census of Agricultural: Puerto Rico Data Release*. June 9, 2020. https://www.nass.usda.gov/Newsroom/Executive_Briefings/2020/06-09-2020.pdf.

US Federal Emergency Management Agency. *Hurricane Maria Update*. Release no. DR-4339-PR NR 046. November 6, 2017. Washington, DC: FEMA. https://www.fema.gov/press-release/20210318/hurricane-maria-update-0.

US General Accounting Office. *Tax Policy: Puerto Rico and the Section 936 Tax Credit*. Report B-253336. Washington, DC: US General Accounting Office, 1993.

Walsh, Catherine. "Decolonial Praxis: Sowing Existence-Life in Times of Dehumanities." Keynote presentation, IX Congress of the International Academy of Practical Theology, Sao Leopoldo, Brazil, April 5, 2019. https://iapt-cs.org/ojs/index.php/iaptcs/article/view/189/624.

Whiteside, H. "Foreign in a Domestic Sense: Puerto Rico's Debt Crisis and Paradoxes in Critical Urban Studies." *Urban Studies* 56, no. 1(2019): 147–66. https://doi.org/10.1177/0042098018768483.

Willison, Charley E., Phillip M. Singer, Melissa S. Creary, and Scott L. Greer. "Quantifying Inequities in US Federal Response to Hurricane Disaster in Texas and Florida Compared with Puerto Rico." *BMJ Global Health* 4, no. 1 (2019). https://gh.bmj.com/content/4/1/e001191.

Young, Rick, Laura Sullivan, Emma Schwartz, and Fritz Kramer. "Blackout in Puerto Rico." *Frontline*, season 2018, episode 10, aired May 1, 2018. https://www.pbs.org/wgbh/frontline/film/blackout. Accessed May 15, 2018.

Zambrana, Rocío. *Colonial Debts: The Case of Puerto Rico*. Durham, NC: Duke University Press, 2021.

INDEX

abandonment, 5, 61, 78; and land loss, 52; by the state, 83, 94

abolition: of accounting, 14; and farming, 85, 91; of prisons, 88

abundance, 80, 115, 131, 135; and scarcity, 119

Act 22: and building occupation, 75; and displacement, 63–64

affirmation: and earth, 132; and freedom, 123; and land, 128

AfroBoricua, 15

Afro-Indigenous, 112, 143n2, 158n3

agile learning methodology, 103, 161n2

agricultura cimarrona (maroon agriculture), 85–86

agroecology, 85, 90. See also beekeeping

Aldarondo, Cecilia, 12, 147n31

aliveness, 7–8, 145n13. See also Quashie, Kevin

Amigxs del M.A.R., 54, 56–57, 153n12

ancestors, 111–12, 114, 130, 137; African, 85; and CEPA, 114; Indigenous, 89, 129; jíbaro, 85; and occupy, 122; in training, 129, 163n6

anticapitalist, 33

antiracist, 84; futures, 91

archipelago, 3–5, 7–8, 12,18; ancient trees, 129; and Airbnb, 65; and beach privatization, 58; and COVID 19, 73; and debt, 46; and diasporic Puerto Ricans, 110, 132; and education budget cuts, 37; the future of, 19–20, 44; and land ownership, 86; and outmigration, 51; realities of, 140; and rematriation, 15–16; selling,

63, 65; and US occupation, 57; and water, ix

Arrecifes Pro Ciudad, 55

asambleas del pueblo (public assemblies), 49

assimilation: as racial project, 16; unlearning, 118

auction, 31; and the concierge class, 28; and Vieques, 31

audit the debt, 25, 26, 44, 102; auditoria ya (audit now), 46

austerity, 37, 41; and the financial crisis of 2008, 6; and Los Comedores Sociales de Puerto Rico, 72; post-Maria, 10; and the state, 39, 49. See also dead university

autogestión, 71, 160n1

autonomy, 37, 80, 160–61; jíbaro, 158n3; and mobilizations, 38, 41; and spirituality, 129

Ayuda Legal, 9, 146n18

Banco Popular, 46

batey, 162n3; and the gender binary, 112

beaches, 152n4; El Campamento Playas del Pueblo, 53; La Coalición Playas Para el Pueblo, 54; and land loss, 52; and lockdown, 125; and privatization, 52, 57, 61. See also archipelago

beekeeping, 87; and agroecological farming methods, 87

black feminist, and the kitchen table, 84. See also brown, adrienne maree

Black Feminist Breathing Chorus, 123

blackout, 106. See also electricity

blood relations, 79–80